Roger Norris and Mike Wooster

Cambridge International AS & A Level

Chemistry

Practical Workbook

CAMBRIDGE
UNIVERSITY PRESS

CAMBRIDGE
UNIVERSITY PRESS

University Printing House, Cambridge CB2 8BS, United Kingdom

One Liberty Plaza, 20th Floor, New York, NY 10006, USA

477 Williamstown Road, Port Melbourne, VIC 3207, Australia

314–321, 3rd Floor, Plot 3, Splendor Forum, Jasola District Centre, New Delhi–110025, India

79 Anson Road, #06–04/06, Singapore 079906

Cambridge University Press is part of the University of Cambridge.

It furthers the University's mission by disseminating knowledge in the pursuit of education, learning and research at the highest international levels of excellence.

Information on this title: www.cambridge.org/ 9781108439046

First published 2018

20 19 18 17 16 15 14 13 12 11 10 9 8 7 6 5 4 3 2 1

Printed in Spain by GraphyCems

A catalogue record for this publication is available from the British Library

ISBN 978-1-108-43904-6 Paperback

....

Acknowledgements (Chemistry Workbook)
Thanks to the following for permission to reproduce images:
Cover isak55/Shutterstock; Fig 4.1a and c GIPhotoStock/SCIENCE PHOTO LIBRARY; Fig 4.1b Charles D. Winters/SCIENCE PHOTO LIBRARY

Contents

1 Introduction   v

2 Safety   vi

3 Skills chapter   vii

1 Masses, moles and atoms
- 1.1 Empirical formula of hydrated copper(II) sulfate crystals   1
- 1.2 Relative atomic mass of magnesium using molar volumes   5
- 1.3 Percentage composition of a mixture of sodium hydrogen carbonate and sodium chloride   9
- 1.4 Relative atomic mass of calcium by two different methods: molar volume and titration   12

2 Structure and bonding
- 2.1 Physical properties of three different types of chemical structure   16
- 2.2 Effect of temperature on the volume of a fixed mass of gas   18
- 2.3 Effect of pressure on the volume of a fixed mass of gas   21

3 Enthalpy changes
- 3.1 Enthalpy change for the reaction between zinc and aqueous copper(II) sulfate solution   24
- 3.2 Enthalpy change of combustion of alcohols   29
- 3.3 Enthalpy change of thermal decomposition   34
- 3.4 Change in enthalpy of hydration of copper (II) sulfate   38

4 Redox reactions
- 4.1 Understanding redox (I): investigating reactivity series and displacement reactions   43
- 4.2 Understanding redox (II): investigating further reactions   47

5 Chemical equilibrium
- 5.1 Applying Le Chatelier's principle to a gaseous equilibrium   52
- 5.2 Applying Le Chatelier's principle to an aqueous equilibrium   54
- 5.3 The equilibrium constant for the hydrolysis of ethyl ethanoate   57

6 Rates of reaction
- 6.1 Effects of concentration on rate of chemical reaction   66
- 6.2 Effects of temperature and a homogeneous catalyst on the rate of chemical reaction   70
- 6.3 Observed catalysed reaction   73

7 The properties of metals
- 7.1 Properties of metal oxides and metal chlorides across Period 3   74
- 7.2 Relative atomic mass of magnesium using a back-titration method   77
- 7.3 Separation of two metal ions in solution   80
- 7.4 Identification of three metal compounds using qualitative analysis   82

8 The properties of non-metals
- 8.1 Formula of hydrated sodium thiosulfate crystals   86
- 8.2 Preparation and properties of the hydrogen halides   89
- 8.3 Reaction of bromine with sulfite (sulfate (IV))   92
- 8.4 Identification of unknowns containing halide ions   95

iii

9 Hydrocarbons and halogenoalkanes

9.1	Cracking of hydrocarbons	98
9.2	How halogenoalkane structure affects the rate of hydrolysis	101

10 Organic compounds containing oxygen

10.1	Identifying four unknown organic compounds	106

11 More about enthalpy changes

11.1	Enthalpy change of vaporisation of water	114
11.2	Enthalpy change of solution of chlorides	118
11.3	Thermal decomposition of iron (II) ethanedioate	123
11.4	Thermal decomposition of metal carbonates	126
11.5	Enthalpy change of mixing	130

12 Electrochemistry

12.1	Determining the Faraday constant	133
12.2	Comparing the voltage of electrochemical cells	137
12.3	Half-cells containing only ions as reactants	139
12.4	Changing the concentration of ions in an electrochemical cell	142
12.5	Electrical conductivity of ethanoic aid	145

13 Further aspects of equilibria

13.1	Change in pH during an acid–base titration	149
13.2	Partition of ammonia between water and trichloromethane	153
13.3	An esterification reaction at equilibrium	156
13.4	The effect of temperature on the $N_2O_4 \rightleftharpoons 2NO_2$ equilibrium	159
13.5	Equilibrium, entropy and enthalpy change	163

14 Reaction kinetics

14.1	Kinetics of the reaction between propanone and iodine	166
14.2	Rate of decomposition of an organic compound	169
14.3	Determination of the order of a reaction	172
14.4	Effect of temperature on rate of reaction	176

15 Transition elements

15.1	Copper content of copper ore	180
15.2	Analysis of iron tablets	183
15.3	Formula of a complex ion	185
15.4	Reaction of copper with potassium dichromate(VI)	188

16 More about organic chemistry

16.1	Making an azo dye	191
16.2	Acylation of a nucleic acid	194
16.3	Nitration of benzene	197

17 Identifying organic compounds

17.1	Extracting an amino acid from hair	200
17.2	Identification of a white crystalline solid	203
17.3	Preparation and identification of a colourless liquid	206

Introduction

Practical work is an essential part of your advanced Chemistry course. Experimental investigations allow you to gain first-hand experience of the arrangement and names of chemical apparatus and how this apparatus is used to obtain meaningful experimental results. For Cambridge International AS & A Level Chemistry Paper 3 and Paper 5 focus on the assessment of practical skills.

The practical investigations in this workbook have been carefully chosen to allow you to practise and improve your practical skills. The practical work introduced in this workbook emphasises the spirit of enquiry and first-hand experience that helps reinforce your knowledge and helps you apply the results and draw conclusions. It also helps you to test your knowledge and application of theoretical work.

The order of the investigations presented largely follows the order of the topics in the Cambridge International AS & A Level Chemistry coursebook. This does not mean that this is the order that will be chosen by your teacher. Some coursebook chapters involve the use of quantitative techniques and when you carry out these investigations you will need calculators and equipment for drawing graphs. All techniques listed in the practical guidance are covered in the workbook.

There are two parts to this practical guide.

The first part deals with subject matter and practical techniques described in the AS level syllabus. A variety of investigations introduces you to a range of experiments which will provide you with practice in manipulating apparatus and taking measurements. Some investigations also ask you to present and analyse data and observations and/or give you practice in drawing conclusions and evaluating information.

The second part deals with subject matter and practical techniques described in the A Level syllabus. This part gives you practice in planning experiments, analysing results, drawing conclusions and evaluating information. The syllabus stresses that 'candidates cannot be adequately prepared for Paper 5 without extensive laboratory work'. With this in mind, some of the investigations give you further practice in laboratory work as well as giving you the opportunity to analyse information, draw conclusions and evaluate the experiment. A number of open-ended investigations have also been included, which give you only the basic information to enable you to plan and carry out an experiment in the laboratory. Other investigations are set in areas of Chemistry that may be new to you or are difficult to investigate experimentally in a school laboratory. In these cases, relevant information is always given so that you can complete the investigations successfully.

The various investigations and accompanying questions will help you gain confidence in tackling laboratory work and develop a wide range of skills related to practical chemistry. Apart from the necessary preparation for both practical papers, it is hoped that these investigations will help you understand the importance of laboratory work in development and assessment of theoretical chemistry.

Safety

Practical work has its own set of skills. A number of these are related to working safely. Working safely is essential in getting the maximum advantage from your practical work.

In each investigation involving practical work, you are expected to:

1 Wear eye protection such as safety goggles or safety spectacles (note that goggles give more protection)
2 Tie back long hair and make sure that items of clothing are tucked in
3 Wear gloves when weighing, pouring or filtering hazardous chemicals.

It is also advisable for you to wear a laboratory coat to protect your clothing from chemical splashes.

All chemicals should be treated as hazardous. If they are spilt on the skin you must wash them off immediately using plenty of water. You may not be aware of the dangers of particular chemicals and therefore using them without safety precautions can lead to unforeseen problems. Remember that you should also think about the hazards of all of the substances that are being produced in a chemical reaction, especially when a gas is given off. Chemical reactions which produce hazardous gases should be done in a fume cupboard or well-ventilated room.

As a learner you should take responsibility for working safely and you must learn the meanings of the safety symbols shown in the table below. Table S1 shows the most common hazard symbols found in school science laboratories. An up-to-date list of CLEAPPS hazards can be downloaded from the internet.

Hazard symbol	What does it mean?	Special points
	The substance is **corrosive**. It will damage your skin and tissues if it comes into contact with them.	Always wear safety goggles and if possible gloves when using corrosive substances
	The substance is an **irritant**. If it comes into contact with your skin it can cause blisters and redness.	Always wear safety spectacles when using irritants.
	The substance is **toxic** and can cause death if swallowed, breathed in or absorbed by skin.	Wear gloves and eye protection.
	The substance is **flammable** and catches fire easily.	Keep the substance away from naked flames and when heating reaction mixtures use the hot water from a kettle rather than using Bunsen burners.
	The material is a **biohazard**. Examples are bacteria and fungi.	Seek advice about particular biohazards.
	The substance is an **oxidising agent**. It will liberate oxygen when heated or in the presence of a suitable catalyst.	Keep oxidising agents well away from flammable materials.

Table S1

Skills chapter

Chapter outline

This chapter introduces the key practical methods, processes and procedures that you will use regularly throughout your course. Within the investigations you'll find cross-references to the techniques covered in this chapter so you are encouraged to refer back to the relevant sections whenever you need to.

This chapter covers the following:

- **Preparing a standard solution**
  - a Calculating the mass of solute required
  - b Making 250cm³ of a standard solution
- **Carrying out an acid–base titration**
  - a preparing the burette
  - b pipetting a solution
  - c carrying out the titration
  - d processing your results
- **Gas collection and measurement**
  - a Choosing your apparatus
  - b General advice for measuring volumes of gases
- **Qualitative analysis: testing for gases and ions**
  - a Tests for gases
  - b Tests for ions

- **Strategies for measuring heat changes**
  - a Temperature–time graphs
  - b Calculating enthalpy (heat) changes
- **Drawing graphs and charts**
- **Calculating errors in your experiments**
  - a Calculating systematic errors due to apparatus inaccuracy
    - i Temperature readings
    - ii Measuring cylinders
    - iii Burette readings
    - iv Top-pan balance readings
- **Using significant figures**

Preparing a standard solution

Introduction

A standard solution is one that has a **known concentration.** With a standard solution, it is possible to investigate the concentration of other solutions of unknown concentration by titration (see section 2). A standard solution is made by dissolving an accurate mass of solute into a known volume of water. The first step is to calculate the mass of solute required to make up a standard solution. For example, if asked to prepare $250\,cm^3$ $(0.25\,dm^3)$ of a $0.100\,mol\,dm^{-3}$ sodium carbonate solution you must first calculate what mass of sodium carbonate you need to weigh out.

In the equations used for calculating amounts and concentrations, the symbols refer to the following quantities:

C = concentration (units = $mol\,dm^{-3}$)

n = number of moles

V = volume (units = dm^3)

m = mass (units = g)

M_r = molar mass (units = $g\,mol^{-1}$)

Please note that not all substances make good standard solutions. This is due to the fact that some substances can be difficult to obtain in a completely pure form, are unstable in air or not readily soluble in water.

a Calculating the mass of solute required

Before you start to prepare your solution you need to calculate the mass of solute you will need to weigh out using the relationships:

$$C = \frac{n}{V} \text{ and } n = \frac{m}{M_r}.$$

The calculations to work out the mass of sodium carbonate ($M_r = 106$) required to prepare 250 cm³ of a 0.100 mol dm⁻³ solution are shown in Figure 0.1

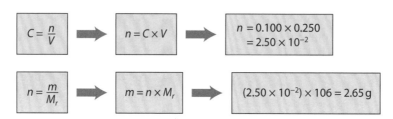

Figure 0.1

b Making 250 cm³ of a standard solution

Equipment

You will need:

- top-pan balance and weighing boat • 250 cm³ beaker • glass or plastic stirring rod
- filter funnel • plastic dropper for delivering small volumes • 250 cm³ volumetric flask
- eye-protection

Access to:

- distilled water in wash bottle • solute

Method

HINT

you must make sure the volume of solution in the volumetric flask **does not go over the mark** on the neck of the volumetric flask

1 Use the weighing boat to weigh out the required amount of solute. Empty it into a 250 cm³ beaker. To ensure there is no solute remaining in the weighing boat, wash the weighing boat twice using distilled water from a wash bottle pouring the washings into the beaker.

2 Add more water to the beaker so that you have about 100 cm³. Stir the mixture with the stirring rod until all the sodium carbonate has dissolved.

3 Place the filter funnel into the neck of the 250 cm³ volumetric flask and pour the contents of the beaker into the flask.

4 Using a wash bottle rinse the beaker and pour the washings into the volumetric flask. Repeat this several times. You must also rinse the stirring rod.

5 When the level of the liquid is just a few cm³ below the mark on the neck of the volumetric flask, take the dropper and **with great care** use it to add distilled water from the wash bottle to the solution one drop at a time until the lowest point of the meniscus is touching the line as shown in Figure 0.2

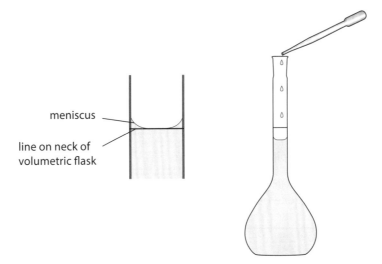

meniscus

line on neck of volumetric flask

Figure 0.2

6   Place the stopper in the neck of the volumetric flask and **keeping the stopper firmly in the neck using your thumb** mix the solution by turning the flask upside down at least five or six times (see Figure 0.3). If you move the flask and still see swirling currents in the liquid you have not mixed enough – just turn upside down a few more times.

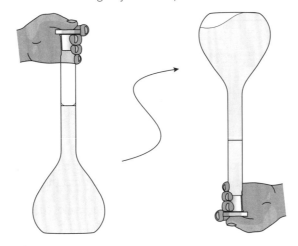

Figure 0.3

Carrying out an acid–base titration

Introduction

Titrations are used to measure the volume of one solution that exactly reacts with another solution. Titration is an analytical technique widely used in industry and is an essential chemical skill. The food industry, for example, uses titrations to determine the amount of salt or sugar in a product or the concentration of beneficial vitamins. Acid–base titrations involve neutralisation between an acid and a base when mixed in solution. An indicator is used to determine the end-point of the titration as it changes colour. This technique is also used in other areas of your syllabus, for example redox reactions.

Additional advice

- When doing acid–base titrations, it is best if the acid is delivered from a burette. This is because alkalis and soluble carbonates can form solids in the taps of burettes and clog them up.

- Burettes should be clamped firmly but not too tightly.

- It is often a good idea to place the burette and clamp stand on a chair or stool. This will make it easier to fill the burette.

- **Never fill a pipette by mouth.** Always use a pipette filler (see Figure 0.5).

- Most pipette fillers have a way of pushing the liquid out of the pipette. Unfortunately, this method is often very difficult to use to the fine level necessary.

Equipment

You will need:

- burette • burette stand or clamp stand • boss and clamp • pipette and pipette filler • white tile • conical flask • 100 cm³ and 250 cm³ beakers • protective gloves • eye protection

Access to:

- distilled water • an indicator (e.g. methyl orange)

---

a preparing the burette

Method

1 Set up the burette in a burette or clamp stand; it should be clamped firmly but not too tightly.

2 Place a filter funnel in the neck of the burette. Close the tap on the burette.

3 Wearing gloves, add some of the acid to a **dry** 100 cm³ beaker. Use the beaker to add a few cm³ of acid to the burette; you are only rinsing the burette at this stage.

4 Open the tap, run out the acid rinse. Ensure the tap is closed, then fill the burette to **above** the zero mark. Remove the funnel from the burette.

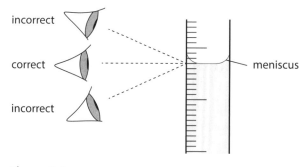

Figure 0.4

HINT

When reading a burette you must always **view it at eye level** as shown in Figure 0.4 so that you accurately record the level of the lowest point of the solution's meniscus

5 Run out some of the acid into the 100 cm³ beaker to ensure the jet at the bottom of the burette is full and there is no air in it. Remove the funnel from the top of the burette.

6 Read and record the starting level of acid in the burette.

b pipetting a solution

A pipette and pipette filler is used to measure out an accurate volume of the alkali or soluble carbonate in an acid–base titration.

Method

1 Pour a volume of the alkali/soluble carbonate into a dry 250 cm³ beaker.

2 Using a pipette filler, fill the pipette (e.g. a 25.0 cm³ pipette) up a little way above the line on the neck. Quickly remove the pipette from the pipette filler and cover the open end with your index (first) finger as shown in Figure 0.5(b).

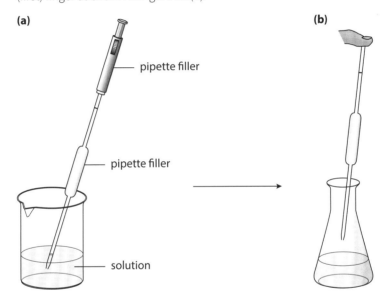

Figure 0.5

3 By releasing your index finger you can now let the solution out of the pipette. When the solution's meniscus is on the line on the neck of the pipette you have exactly 25.0 cm³ of solution in the pipette.

4 The solution can now be transferred to the conical flask. When the end of the pipette is over the conical flask release your index finger and let the solution run into the flask.

c carrying out the titration

Now that you have your burette prepared and filled with acid and an accurate amount of your alkali/soluble carbonate in a conical flask, you are ready to start your acid/base titration. You will need to repeat the titration at least three times, usually more. The first titration is a rough titration which will help you to be more accurate when you repeat the process. You will need to prepare a results table in which to record your results.

1 Place the conical flask on a white tile directly under the outlet of the burette.

2 Add 2–3 drops of the indicator provided.

3 Remember that the first titration is a **rough** titration. You will add acid from the burette $1.00\,cm^3$ at a time. After each addition, swirl the flask and if the indicator does not change colour continue adding $1.00\,cm^3$ at a time until it does.

4 Note the volume of the acid added. What does this result tell you? If the indicator changed colour after $24.00\,cm^3$ of acid was added then you know that the end-point of the titration was somewhere between 23.00 and $24.00\,cm^3$. You now know that you can safely run in $23.00\,cm^3$ of acid from the burette without the indicator changing colour.

5 Wash out the conical flask with plenty of tap water and then rinse with distilled water ready for your second titration.

6 Using the pipette add another $25.00\,cm^3$ of the solution of the base to the flask and add another 2–3 drops of indicator.

7 At the point when you have added $1\,cm^3$ less than the volume recorded in your rough titration, you now need to add one drop of acid at a time, swirling the conical flask as you do so. When you are near the end-point, the colour of the indicator will take longer to return to its original colour. As soon as the colour does not change back you know you have added exactly the right amount of acid. Note down the volume.

8 Wash out the conical flask with plenty of tap water and then rinse with distilled water ready for your third titration. If you have enough acid left in your burette to repeat the titration, go ahead; if not you will need to fill the burette up again (taking care to record the starting level) and then repeat.

9 Continue to repeat the method until you have **at least two concordant (consistent) results**. Then you will know that you have accurately estimated the volume of acid required to react with the $25.00\,cm^3$ of your alkali/soluble carbonate.

d processing your results

Before completing calculations using your results you need to check and process your results to determine the average titre.

Figure 0.6 and Table 0.1 provide sample burette readings and a results table which are reviewed.

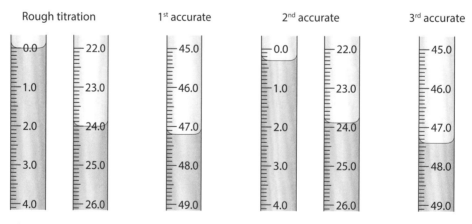

Figure 0.6

> **HINT**
> Remember that you don't have to adjust the level of acid in the burette to exactly $0.00\,cm^3$ as this is time consuming and unnecessary; just record the exact starting level in the burette

	Rough titration/ cm³	First accurate titration/cm³	Second accurate titration/cm³	Third accurate titration/cm³
Final burette reading	24.00	47.20	23.90	47.40
Initial burette reading	0.00	24.00	0.30	23.90
Titre /cm³	24.00	23.20	23.60	23.50

Table 0.1

Review of readings and results:

- The results are recorded to two decimal places but this is not because the burette can be read to 0.01 cm³. The burette is accurate to ±0.05 cm³.

- The initial burette reading is usually recorded on the second line of the table to aid the calculation of the titre.

- The initial burette reading for the second accurate titration is 0.30 cm³. Note that no time was wasted in adjusting the volume to 0.00 cm³. In this titration, acid was added until a reading of 23.30 cm³ before then being added drop by drop.

- **Three** accurate titrations were necessary because the first two titre values were not close enough in value (concordant).

- The titres for the second and third accurate titrations were concordant so there was no need to do any further titrations.

- The average titre was calculated using the second and third accurate titrations:

$$\frac{23.60 - 23.50}{2} = 23.55 \text{ cm}^3$$

Gas collection and measurement

Introduction

You can investigate a chemical reaction by measuring the volume of gas given off (evolved) at certain time intervals (when investigating reaction rates), or measuring the total volume of gas produced. There are different techniques to collect gas during an experiment and your choice of apparatus depends on the volume of gas produced and the apparatus that is available. The gas produced must be only slightly soluble or insoluble in water.

a Choosing your apparatus

Two common methods for collecting gas are shown in Figure 0.7. In (a) the gas produced is collected in a gas syringe. In (b) the gas is collected by the displacement of water. It is a suitable method for gases that are insoluble in water such as hydrogen.

It is important to have some idea of the volume of gas that will be generated during your experiment so that you can choose an appropriate size of syringe or measuring cylinder. The volume of measuring cylinder chosen should be about 2–3 times the volume of gas.

Remember that the larger the volume of measuring cylinder that you use, the greater the error in measurement (e.g. if the volume to be collected is 12 cm³ then the ideal size of measuring cylinder is 25 cm³).

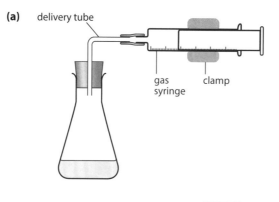

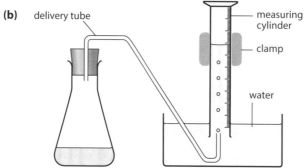

Figure 0.7

b General advice for measuring volumes of gases

- After selecting your apparatus it will be necessary to complete a range of measurements. Trial runs are therefore essential to make sure that your approach will work.

Example 1

When asked to investigate the effect of concentration of hydrochloric acid (e.g. 0.100–2.00 $mol\,dm^{-3}$) on magnesium ribbon, you would collect gas using the displacement of water (Figure 0.7 (b)).

- It is advisable to complete trial runs using the lowest and highest values of your range that you intend to use in your experiment (e.g. in Example 1, you would use the lowest and highest acid concentrations: 0.100 and 2.00 $mol\,dm^{-3}$). This will indicate which size of measuring cylinder is correct to use.

- When you are measuring the volume at different times it can be easily read at the correct time if you start reading the volume a few seconds before the required time and count down.

Qualitative analysis: testing for gases and ions

Introduction

Knowing how to identify different ions and gases is a key skill for all chemists. In particular it is important to understand the chemical basis for each test. The practical exam will test your knowledge of common tests and their expected results.

a Tests for gases.

After collecting gas during an experiment, it will be necessary to complete a test to establish what gas you have. The tests for common gases (and the method used in the testing) are shown in Table 0.2.

Gas	Test and result	Method
Carbon dioxide (CO_2)	Bubble gas through limewater (calcium hydroxide) solution. Turns cloudy in presence of CO_2.	Using dropper, collect gas from above the surface of the reaction mixture; bubble gas through limewater solution.
Hydrogen (H_2)	Use lighted splint. H_2 produces squeaky 'pop' when burnt.	Collect gas in upside down test tube above reaction mixture. Then insert lighted splint into test tube.
Oxygen (O_2)	Use glowing splint. O_2 relights glowing splint.	Collect gas using displacement of water. Insert glowing splint into the measuring cylinder.
Ammonia (NH_3)	Universal Indicator (UI) or red litmus paper. NH_3 turns moist UI or red litmus paper blue/purple.	Hold indicator paper at mouth of test tube. Must be carried out in a fume cupboard.
Chlorine (Cl_2)	Universal Indicator (UI) or blue litmus paper. Chlorine gas bleaches moist UI or blue litmus paper.	Hold indicator paper at mouth of test tube. Must be carried out in a fume cupboard.
Sulfur dioxide (SO_2)	Acidified potassium manganate(VII) solution. SO_2 decolourises acidified potassium manganate(VII) solution on filter paper.	Add 2–3 drops of potassium manganate(VII) solution to filter paper and hold near mouth of test tube. Must be carried out in a fume cupboard.

Table 0.2

b Tests for ions

When presented with a substance or solid to analyse it may be necessary to first prepare a solution of the compound. Here is some general advice regarding the making and testing of solutions.

1   Do not be tempted to make your solution too concentrated

2   When testing for ions it is sensible to add the test solution a drop at a time

3   When testing for anions you must first add the appropriate acid before the testing solution.

Example 1
When testing for halide ions you use silver nitrate solution. But before adding the silver nitrate solution, you add **nitric acid**.

Example 2
When testing for sulfate ions you use barium chloride solution. But before adding the barium chloride solution, you add a drop or two of **hydrochloric acid**, but sulfate ions (SO_4^{2-}) can be distinguished from sulfite (SO_3^{2-}) ions by first adding the barium chloride and then adding the hydrochloric acid.

Strategies for measuring heat changes

Introduction

One of the main challenges when taking measurements of heat change is avoiding heat loss, mainly by conduction and convection. There is also the issue that should the reaction take a long time to go to completion then the maximum temperature may not be reached. Ideally there would be no heat loss; the reaction would take place immediately and it would be possible to measure the temperature immediately.

In order to overcome these challenges it is necessary when investigating heat change to construct a temperature–time graph

a Temperature–time graphs

A typical temperature–time graph is shown in Figure 0.8.

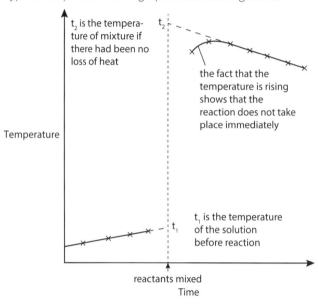

Figure 0.8

The experiment shown in Figure 0.8 was conducted and measurements, which were later plotted, were recorded as follows:

1   The temperature of the reacting solution was measured each minute for the first 4 min.

2   On the fifth minute the temperature was not measured; the reactants were mixed by stirring them together.

3   On the sixth minute the temperature was measured and every minute afterwards for as long as it was deemed necessary (in this case for a further 6 min).

Review Figure 0.8. You can see that the first four measurements are plotted but that the temperature of the reaction mixture at 5 min is obtained by extrapolating the line to the vertical line at 5 min. Similarly, after 5 min the temperature at 5 min is obtained by extrapolating back to the line at 5 min.

The temperature change = $t_2 - t_1$.

b Calculating enthalpy (heat) changes

HINT

Enthalpy change is the heat change at constant pressure

The enthalpy change produced by a reaction in a solution is represented by the following formula:

$$q = m \times c \times \Delta T$$

Unit = Joules (J)

Where m = mass of solution being heated up or cooled down, c = specific heat capacity of the solution and ΔT = temperature change.

Usually a solution being heated or cooled is an aqueous solution. The mass of solution (g) is therefore assumed equal to the volume (cm³).

This is because under the conditions of the experiment it is **assumed** that the density of water = exactly $1.00\,g\,cm^{-3}$.

The value of c for water = $4.18\,J\,g^{-1}\,K^{-1}$ and it is **assumed** that the value of the solution has the same value.

Example 1
If $50\,cm^3$ of water is heated up by 8 °C (≡ an 8 °K increase) then the enthalpy change is calculated as follows:

$$q = 50 \times 4.18 \times 8\,J = 1672\,J$$

$$= 1.67\,kJ \text{ (three significant figures)}$$

Drawing graphs and charts

Introduction

Drawing accurate graphs and charts is often an essential part of the analysis of experiments. There are many occasions within this workbook when you are asked to first record experimental data and then produce a graph. Here are some general tips and advice to remember:

1 Bar charts (see Figure 0.9(a)) are used to present categorical variables while line graphs (see Figure 0.9(b)) are used for continuous variables.

Example 1
If you are investigating the effect of surface area on the rate of a chemical reaction you might complete an experiment to compare a solid or powder form of a substance on the volume of gas produced in 1 min.

As lumps or powder are categorical variables you would express the results as a bar chart (see Figure 0.9(a)).

Example 2
If you are investigating the effect of concentration on the rate of a reaction then concentration can have any value and is therefore a continuous variable.

Your results would be presented as a line graph (see Figure 0.9(b)).

1 Whether a bar chart or line graph, make sure you use at least $\frac{3}{4}$ of the available grid provided.

2 When plotting two variables, plot the independent variable on the horizontal axis (x-axis) and the dependent variable on the vertical axis (y-axis).

3 After plotting the individual points on a line graph, you are often asked to drawn a best-fit line (see Figure 0.9(b)). If the line is obviously a curve then do not draw a 'point-to-point' line. The curve must be a smooth curve through the points.

4 Points lying well away from this best-fit line are 'anomalous' and not taken into consideration.

5 In many investigations, a zero value for your independent variable will obviously give a zero value for your dependent variable. One point you can be certain of is (0,0) and your best-fit line must go through the origin.

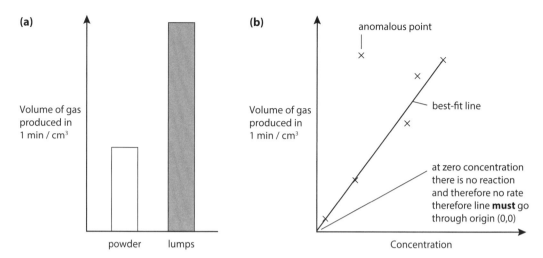

Figure 0.9

Calculating errors in your experiments

Introduction

There are several reasons why the final value that you record during an experiment may be inaccurate. Some of the errors associated with a value may be random (e.g. the substances used may be impure). More commonly though, errors are systematic and are associated with the apparatus that you've used.

For every experiment you complete you must assess and state the total percentage error associated with the values you report.

In some circumstances you can check what the actual value should be. If you know this value then you can calculate the experimental error using the following formula:

$$\text{Percentage error} = \frac{|\text{Actual} - \text{experimental}|}{\text{Actual}} \times 100\%$$

The | sign in this equation reflects the fact that the value being calculated is the absolute value and is always positive.

Example 1
When determining the relative atomic mass of magnesium, the accepted value is 24.3 g mol⁻¹. Your experimental determination gives the value of 26.6 g mol⁻¹.

The percentage error is therefore: $\dfrac{|24.3 - 26.6|}{24.3} = \dfrac{2.3}{24.3} \times 100\% = 9.47\%$

More commonly you need to calculate the total percentage error by adding up the percentage errors inherent in the apparatus you've used.

The overall **percentage error** will depend on the apparatus which has the greatest percentage error.

a Calculating systematic errors due to apparatus inaccuracy

i Temperature readings

A thermometer can have an uncertainty of ±1 °C.

In the same experiment, if you take two temperature readings and the first one gives you a reading of 21 °C and the second one gives you a reading of 42 °C then the temperature rise is 21 °C.

However, due to the inaccuracy inherent in the apparatus we know that the lower reading is 21±1 °C so could be as low as 20 °C or as high as 22 °C. Similarly, the second reading could be as high as 43 °C or as low as 41 °C.

The maximum difference is therefore 23 °C and the minimum difference is 19 °C.

The true reading is therefore 21±2°.

The percentage error = $(\dfrac{\text{Maximum error}}{\text{Value of measurement}})$ x 100 % = $\dfrac{2}{21}$ x 100 % = 9.52 %.

ii Measuring cylinders

Measuring cylinders are accurate to ±1 cm³.

It you measure out 50.0 cm³ of a solution in a 100 cm³ cylinder

The percentage error = $\dfrac{1}{50}$ x 100 % = 2 %.

iii Burette readings

Burettes used in schools usually read to ±0.05 cm³.

If you make two burette readings in a titration then each of them has an error of ±0.05 cm⁻³ and the total error is therefore 0.10 cm³.

If you run in 22 cm³ of solution,

the percentage error = $(\dfrac{\text{Maximum error}}{\text{Value of measurement}})$ x 100 % = $\dfrac{0.10}{22}$ x 100 % = 0.45 %

iv Top-pan balance readings

The maximum error of a top-pan balance will depend on the quality of the balance.

The error of an electronic device is usually half of the last precision digit.

The accuracy of a two decimal place balance is ±0.005 g. Each reading has this error and if you make two readings then the maximum error is ±0.01 g.

Example 2
Mass of weighing boat + solid = 10.34 g   Maximum error = 0.005 g

Mass of weighing boat = 10.00 g   Maximum error = 0.005 g

Mass of solid = 0.34 g   Maximum error = 0.01 g

The percentage error = $(\dfrac{\text{Maximum error}}{\text{Value of measurement}})$ x 100 % = $\dfrac{0.01}{0.34}$ x 100 % = 2.94 %

Using significant figures

Introduction

When you note the value of a result you need to be very aware of the amount of significant figures you use. The correct number of significant figures depends on the apparatus you use and the number of significant figures quoted for each measurement.

Example 1
In an investigation involving the use of a top-pan balance, burettes and thermometers:

The mass quoted in the results is 9.76 g

The measurement of solution from the burette was 25.00 cm³

The temperature is quoted as 7.4 °C.

The measurement quoted to the lowest number of significant figures is the temperature. That is to two significant figures. This means that your final result should also be quoted to two significant figures.

Please note that the final result should be rounded down to two significant figures, but that this should be done right at the very end of your calculation. If you round down too early then you'll introduce a rounding error.

Chapter 1:
Masses, moles and atoms

Chapter outline

This chapter relates to Chapter 1: Moles and equations, Chapter 2: Atomic structure and Chapter 3: Electrons in atoms in the coursebook.

In this chapter you will complete investigations on:

- 1.1 Empirical formula of hydrated copper(II) sulfate crystals
- 1.2 Relative atomic mass of magnesium using molar volumes
- 1.3 Percentage composition of a mixture of sodium hydrogen carbonate and sodium chloride
- 1.4 Relative atomic mass of calcium by two different methods: molar volume and titration

Practical investigation 1.1:
Empirical formula of hydrated copper(II) sulfate crystals

Introduction

In this investigation you will determine the empirical formula (refer to Chapter 1 of the coursebook if required) of hydrated copper(II) sulfate by finding the value of **x** in $CuSO_4.\mathbf{x}H_2O$. You will weigh out some hydrated copper(II) sulfate in an evaporating basin, heat it to constant mass, determine the mass of water present in your sample and then find the molar ratio $CuSO_4 : H_2O$.

Equipment

You will need:

• a pipe-clay triangle • an evaporating basin • Bunsen burner and tripod • tongs • glass stirring rod • two heat-resistant pads • spatula

Access to:

• a supply of gas • a top-pan balance that reads to at least two decimal places

---

Safety considerations

- Make sure you have read the advice in the Safety section at the beginning of this book and listen to any advice from your teacher before carrying out this investigation.

- You must wear eye protection at all times in this experiment and tie your hair back if it is long.

- Copper(II) sulfate is an irritant and is harmful if swallowed.

- Carry the evaporating basin to the top-pan balance on a heat-resistant pad. Do not use the tongs to carry it.

Method

1   Weigh an empty evaporating basin and then weigh the mass of crystals that you have been given.

Mass of basin + $CuSO_4.xH_2O$ crystals . . . . .g

Mass of basin . . . . .g

Mass of $CuSO_4.xH_2O$ crystals .g

2   Place the pipe-clay triangle and the evaporating basin containing your crystals on the tripod as shown in Figure. 1.1.

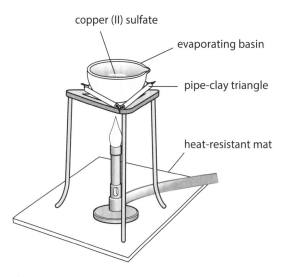

copper (II) sulfate

evaporating basin

pipe-clay triangle

heat-resistant mat

Figure 1.1

3   Copper(II) sulfate decomposes if heated too strongly. Heat the crystals **very gently**. A low, just-blue Bunsen flame should be used for this.

4   While you are heating the crystals, stir them using the glass stirring rod. At the same time grip the evaporating basin using the tongs to prevent the evaporating basin toppling over and spilling the contents.

5   At first, the copper(II) sulfate will be 'sticky' but after a short amount of time it should not cling to the glass rod and will become powdery.

6   The colour of the copper(II) sulfate will change from blue to light blue and then to a very light grey, almost white.

7   When it gets to this stage weigh the evaporating basin and anhydrous copper(II) sulfate.

Mass of basin + copper(II) sulfate = ...g

8   Reheat the powder for a short while and then reweigh it. If constant mass is obtained, then all the water of crystallisation will have been driven off from the crystals.

Mass of basin + copper(II) sulfate =. . . . . .g

9   If the mass has decreased, then keep on reheating and reweighing until a constant mass is obtained.

Repeat (1) Mass of basin + copper(II) sulfate =. . . . . .g

Repeat (2) Mass of basin + copper(II) sulfate =. . . . . .g

Repeat (3) Mass of basin + copper(II) sulfate =. . . . . .g

HINT

Note when cool, anhydrous $CuSO_4$ absorbs water from the air

2

Data analysis

a Calculate the mass of the anhydrous copper(II) sulfate remaining and then the mass of water that has been lost from the crystals on heating. This is the water of crystallisation.

Mass of anhydrous $CuSO_4$ =................g

Mass of water of crystallisation =................g

b Using the grid supplied, draw a set of axes with mass of anhydrous copper(II) sulfate on the horizontal (x) axis and mass of the water of crystallisation on the vertical (y) axis. Use suitable scales and label the axes.

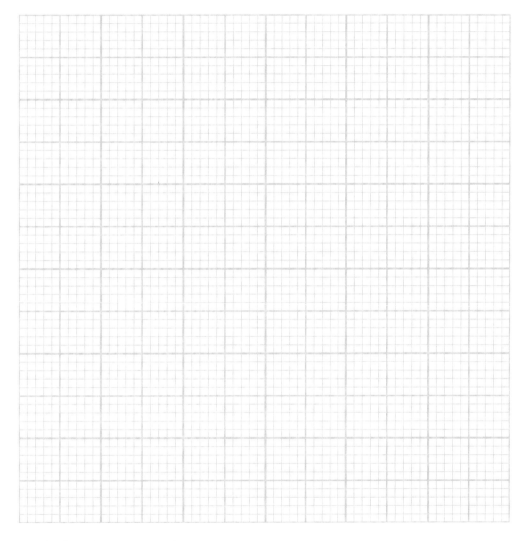

HINT

Remember your line must go through the origin

- Plot the points on the graph.
- Reject any points that are obviously wrong.
- Draw a best-fit line through the points.

c Use your line to calculate the mass of water that combines with 1.60 g of anhydrous copper(II) sulfate ($CuSO_4$)

Mass of water =....................g

3

d   From your result, calculate the number of moles of water that combine with one mole of $CuSO_4$.

....

....

....

e   Calculate the value of x in the formula $CuSO_4.xH_2O$

x = ...

Evaluation

f   Which point should you be most confident about?

Explain your answer.

....

....

....

> **HINT**
>
> If the point lies above the line, the ratio of water to anhydrous copper(II) sulfate is greater than it should be

g   Explain any points:

i   that lie **above** your best-fit line.

....

....

....

ii   that lie **below** your best-fit line.

....

....

....

> **HINT**
>
> If the point lies below the line, the ratio of water to anhydrous copper(II) sulfate is less than it should be

h   Copper(II) sulfate crystals lose their water of crystallisation between 100 °C and 350 °C. They start to decompose at approximately 600 °C.

Briefly describe a better way of heating the copper(II) sulfate crystals in this experiment and explain why it is an improvement on the method you used.

....

....

....

4

Practical investigation 1.2:
Relative atomic mass of magnesium using molar volumes

Introduction

The objective of this investigation is to find the relative atomic mass of magnesium using its reaction with dilute hydrochloric acid to give hydrogen gas.

Refer back to Chapter 1 Moles and equations of the coursebook for more details of the theory.

The equation for the reaction between magnesium and hydrochloric acid is:

$$Mg(s) + 2HCl(aq) \rightarrow MgCl_2(aq) + H_2(g)$$

1 mol of any gas occupies 24 000 cm³ (at room temperature and pressure)

This reaction can be used to find the relative atomic mass of magnesium. By determining the number of moles of hydrogen produced by a known mass of magnesium (m), the number of moles (n) of magnesium can be determined.

The relative atomic mass of magnesium can then be found using $A_r = \dfrac{m}{n}$.

As the masses of short lengths of magnesium ribbon are very small and difficult to measure on a top-pan balance, you will measure out a 10 cm length and weigh it. You will then estimate the masses of different shorter lengths and use these for your experiments.

Equipment

You will need:

• apparatus for collection and measurement of gas • small piece of steel wool • one 10.0 cm length of magnesium ribbon • 30 cm ruler • plastic gloves (see safety considerations)
• scissors

Access to:

• a top-pan balance reading to **at least** two decimal place • 2 mol dm⁻³ hydrochloric acid

---

Safety considerations

• Make sure you have read the advice in the Safety section at the beginning of this book and listen to any advice from your teacher before carrying out this investigation.

• You must wear eye protection at all times in this experiment.

• Magnesium is highly flammable.

• Hydrogen is a flammable gas.

• 2 mol dm⁻³ hydrochloric acid is an irritant.

• Steel wool sometimes splinters so use gloves if you have sensitive skin.

• If you are using a glass measuring cylinder for collecting the gas or a gas syringe then take care when clamping it because over-tightening of the clamp could shatter the glass.

Method

1 Take a 10.0 cm length of magnesium ribbon and **gently** clean it by using the steel wool.

2 Weigh the cleaned magnesium ribbon and record its mass.

   Mass of ribbon…………..g

3 Cut the ribbon up into 2 x 0.5 cm, 2 x 1.0 cm, 2 x 1.5 cm and 2 x 2.0 cm lengths.

4 From your mass for 10.0 cm of ribbon, estimate the mass of the 1.0 cm, 1.5 cm and 2.0 cm lengths.

Estimated mass of 1.0 cm lengths ....g

Estimated mass of 1.5 cm lengths....................g

Estimated mass of 2.0 cm lengths ....g

5 Depending on which gas collecting system you are going to use, set up your apparatus as shown in Figure 1.2.

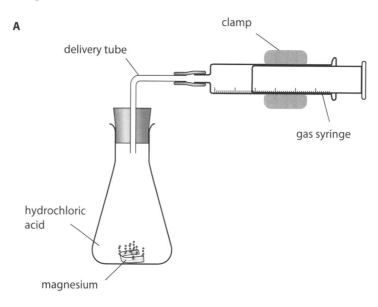

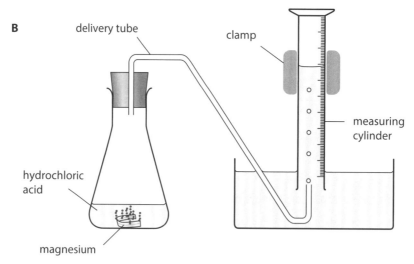

Figure 1.2

6 Measure out 25.0 cm³ of hydrochloric acid into the conical flask.

    a Set up the apparatus ready for measurement of a gas.

    b Add one of the 1 cm lengths of magnesium ribbon to the acid, quickly replace the bung and start collecting the gas.

    c Continuously swirl the flask because the magnesium will stick to the sides of the flask.

    d When the reaction is finished, record the volume of gas produced.

      Volume of gas given by a 1.0 cm length of ribbon = ... cm³

7 Repeat Step 6 with all the other known lengths of magnesium ribbon.

Volume of gas (from 1.0 cm of ribbon)...............................cm³

Volume of gas (from 1.5 cm of ribbon)...............................cm³

Volume of gas (from 1.5 cm of ribbon)...............................cm³

Volume of gas (from 2.0 cm of ribbon)...............................cm³

Volume of gas (from 2.0 cm of ribbon)...............................cm³

Results

Use Table 1.1 to record the mass of the ribbon used and the volumes of hydrogen produced.

Length of Mg ribbon/cm	Mass of Mg/g	Volume of gas produced/cm³		
		Experiment 1	Experiment 2	Average
0.5 cm				
1.0 cm				
1.5 cm				
2.0 cm				

Table 1.1

Data analysis

a Plot a graph of mass of magnesium along the horizontal axis (x-axis) against volume of gas up the vertical axis (y-axis). You should use at least $\frac{3}{4}$ of the space available on the graph.

- Discard any results that are obviously wrong.
- Draw a best-fit line through your points.

b Using your graph, calculate the mass of magnesium that gives 24.0 cm³ of hydrogen gas.

....

....

....

c From this value, calculate the number of moles of magnesium that give this volume of gas and use $A_r = \dfrac{\text{mass of magnesium}}{\text{number of moles}}$ to find the relative atomic mass of magnesium. Assume that under the conditions of the experiment, 1 mol of gas occupies 24 dm³ or 24 000 cm³.

....

....

....

....

d Compare your value for A_r with the value given in your Periodic Table.

Using the following formula, calculate the percentage error in your result.

$$\text{Percentage error} = \frac{|\text{Actual value} - \text{experimental value}|}{\text{Actual value}} \times 100$$

....

....

....

8

HINT

Look back at the Skills chapter for how to calculate the percentage error from your readings

e What was the maximum error for the top-pan balance that you used?

$$\text{The percentage error for your weighing} = \frac{\text{maximum error}}{\text{mass weighed out}} \times 100\%$$

f The percentage error from your measurements of lengths of magnesium ribbon.

....

....

g Using this information, calculate the total error from your length measurements. Remember, you did one weighing but several volume and length measurements and these should be added up.

i Calculated error from length measurements:

....

....

HINT

The ruler measures to 1 mm and the maximum error is ± 0.5 mm or 0.05 cm. Therefore, a 2 cm length is really 2.0 ± 0.05 mm and the percentage error $= \dfrac{0.05}{2.0} \times 100\%$ $= 2.5\%$

ii   Possible errors from volume measurements:

....

....

....

....

iii   Total possible percentage error from apparatus readings:

....

....

....

Evaluation

h   What other factors could limit the accuracy of your results and contribute to the error?

....

....

....

9

Practical investigation 1.3:
Percentage composition of a mixture of sodium hydrogen carbonate and sodium chloride

Introduction

In this practical, you will investigate the percentage composition of a mixture of sodium hydrogen carbonate and sodium chloride using an acid–base titration.

Equipment

You will need:

- a 150 cm³ conical flask • a 250 cm³ volumetric flask • wash bottle of distilled water
- burette stand • a 25 cm³ pipette • white tile • a 250 cm³ beaker and 100 cm³ beaker
- stirring rod • small dropper • small filter funnel for burette and larger one for volumetric flask • a 50 cm³ burette • weighing boat

Access to:

- a top-pan balance reading to two or ideally three decimal places • a mixture of sodium hydrogen carbonate and sodium chloride • 0.100 mol dm⁻³ hydrochloric acid • methyl orange indicator and dropper • distilled water

---

Safety considerations

- Make sure you have read the advice in the Safety section at the beginning of this book and listen to any advice from your teacher before carrying out this investigation.
- Eye protection must be worn at all times in this investigation.
- The hydrochloric acid is an irritant.
- Methyl orange is poisonous. If you get it on your skin, wash it off immediately.

Method

Part 1: Making up the solution of the mixture

1 Weigh out 1.90–2.10 g of the mixture of sodium hydrogen carbonate and sodium chloride.

   Weight of mixture ………………………g

2 Dissolve this solid sample in distilled water and make up to a total volume of 250 cm³ in your volumetric flask as described in the Skills chapter.

Part 2: The titrations

1 Titrate 25 cm³ samples of this solution against the standard 0.100 mol dm⁻³ hydrochloric acid. Use methyl orange as the indicator.

2 You should look back at the Skills chapter for how to do this.

Results

Complete Table 1.2.

	Rough titration/cm³	First accurate titration/cm³	Second accurate titration/cm³	Third accurate titration/cm³
Final burette reading/cm³				
Starting burette reading/cm³				
Titre/cm³				

Table 1.2

Data analysis

a Identify the concordant titres and give the average of these values.

Concordant titres = …………………cm³ and …………………cm³

Average of concordant titres = …………………cm³

Using the data you've collected, you can calculate the number of moles of the sodium hydrogen carbonate present in your sample. You can then calculate the mass of this compound and from that, the composition of the mixture.

The equation for the reaction between hydrochloric acid and sodium hydrogen carbonate is shown below.

$$NaHCO_3(aq) + HCl(aq) \rightarrow NaCl(aq) + CO_2(g) + H_2O(l)$$

b Calculate:

    i The volume of $0.100 \, mol \, dm^{-3}$ hydrochloric acid needed to react completely with the sodium hydrogen carbonate present in $25 \, cm^3$ of the mixture = ...cm^3

    ii The number of moles of hydrochloric acid reacting =................. × ....mol = number of moles of sodium hydrogen carbonate present in $25.00 \, cm^3$ of solution = ...mol

    iii Mass of sodium hydrogen carbonate present (Remember $m = n \times M_r$) = ...g

    iv Total mass of mixture = ...g

    v Therefore, mass of sodium chloride present in mixture = ...g

    vi Percentage of sodium hydrogen carbonate present in mixture = ...%

    vii What is the actual percentage composition of the mixture? (Ask your teacher/supervisor.) Answer = ...%

c You should also calculate the percentage error in your results as you did in Investigation 1.2.

$$\text{Percentage error} = \frac{|\text{Actual value} - \text{experimental value}|}{\text{Actual value}} \times 100$$

Evaluation

d Identify and calculate the systematic errors in your experiment from the following apparatus:

    i The top-pan balance

    ....

    ....

    ii The pipette

    ....

    ....

    iii The burette readings

    ....

    ....

e Identify the random errors in your experiment.

....

....

f What was the main contribution (if any) to your percentage error?

....

....

g How could this be overcome?

....

....

HINT

Remember in each titration you take two readings, each with a possible error of $\pm 0.05 \, cm^3$. So, for example, a titre of $20.00 \, cm^3$ has a maximum possible error of $\pm 0.10 \, cm^3$

Practical investigation 1.4:
Relative atomic mass of calcium by two different methods: molar volume and titration

Introduction

The equation for the reaction between calcium and water is shown below:

$$Ca(s) + 2H_2O(l) \rightarrow Ca(OH)_2(aq) + H_2(g)$$

This reaction can be used to find the relative atomic mass of calcium by finding the number of moles of hydrogen produced by a known mass of calcium. The number of moles of calcium (n) can then be calculated using the relative atomic mass calculated using $A_r = m/n$.

The calcium hydroxide formed in the reaction can then be titrated against standard hydrochloric acid.

Equipment

You will need:

• apparatus for measuring gas volumes as used in Investigation 1.2 • small filter funnel for burette • 50.00 cm³ burette • weighing boat • 150 cm³ conical flask • wash bottle of distilled water • burette stand • 25.00 cm³ pipette • white tile • 250 cm³ beaker • 25.0 cm³ measuring cylinder • methyl orange indicator in dropper bottle

Access to:

• top-pan balance reading to **at least** two decimal places • 0.200 mol dm⁻³ hydrochloric acid • **fresh** calcium granules • distilled water

---

Safety considerations

• Make sure you have read the advice in the Safety section at the beginning of this book and listen to any advice from your teacher before carrying out this investigation.

• You must wear eye protection at all times in this experiment.

• Calcium reacts vigorously with water. Do not handle it with bare hands.

• Hydrogen is a flammable gas.

• 0.2 mol dm⁻³ hydrochloric acid is an irritant.

• If you are using a glass measuring cylinder for collecting the gas or a gas syringe, then take care when clamping it. Over-tightening of the clamp could shatter the glass.

• The calcium hydroxide is an alkali and should be regarded as being corrosive. If you get any on your skin then wash it off immediately.

Part 1: Determination by molar volume

Method

1   Set up your apparatus for reacting the calcium with water and collecting the gas formed during the reaction. Use either of the two arrangements shown in Figure 1.2.

2   Measure out 25 cm³ of distilled water and add to the conical flask.

3   Weigh out between 0.040 g and 0.080 g of calcium.

4   Make sure that your gas collection apparatus is ready.

5 Add the calcium granules to the conical flask and quickly replace the stopper. Swirl the flask vigorously to make sure that all the calcium has reacted.

6 When the reaction is finished note the volume of gas evolved and record it in Table 1.3.

Results

Mass of calcium/g	Volume of hydrogen/cm³	Burette reading for hydrochloric acid/cm³	
		2nd	
		1st	
		Titre	
		2nd	
		1st	
		Titre	
		2nd	
		1st	
		Titre	

Table 1.3

Data analysis

a Assume that 1 mol of gas occupies 24 000 cm³ at room temperature and pressure.

   i Calculate the number of moles of hydrogen formed in your first experiment.

   ii From this, calculate the number of moles of calcium.

   iii Calculate the relative atomic mass of calcium.

....

....

....

....

....

Evaluation

b Using the value shown on your Periodic Table, calculate the percentage error in your result.

$$\text{Percentage error} = \frac{|\text{Actual value} - \text{experimental value}|}{\text{Actual value}} \times 100$$

....

....

c Systematic errors: calculate the percentage errors in your apparatus.

   i The weighing out of the calcium.

....

....

ii The measurement of gas volume.

....

....

iii Random errors: identify the random errors in the method.

....

....

iv Are there any improvements you would make to this method?

....

....

Part 2: Determination by titration

Method

1 Remove the flask from the gas collection apparatus and wash any liquid and white solid on the sides into the solution.

2 **a** Fill up your burette to near the zero mark with $0.200 \, mol \, dm^{-3}$ hydrochloric acid.

b Place a white tile under the burette.

c Add a few drops of methyl orange indicator to the calcium hydroxide in the conical flask. **There are no opportunities for a rough titration**.

3 **a** Add the acid to the flask and after each addition swirl the flask vigorously.

b When the indicator shows signs of colour change to orange red, add the acid more slowly – a drop at a time until an orange colour is obtained.

c Note the new burette reading.

4 **a** Wash the flask thoroughly with tap water and then rinse with distilled water.

b Repeat steps in the two experiments with a new mass of calcium.

> **HINT**
> Look back at Skills chapter for full details on carrying out titrations

Results

Complete Table 1.4

Mass of calcium/g	Volume of hydrogen/cm³	Burette reading for hydrochloric acid/cm³	
		2nd	
		1st	
		Titre	
		2nd	
		1st	
		Titre	
		2nd	
		1st	
		Titre	

Table 1.4

Data analysis

d Calculate the number of moles of hydrochloric acid reacting with the calcium hydroxide.

    i From this value, calculate the number of moles of calcium hydroxide and therefore the number of moles of calcium.

    ii Calculate the relative atomic mass of calcium.

       Repeat these calculations if you have more than one set of results.

....

....

....

....

....

Evaluation

e Using the value shown on your Periodic Table, calculate the percentage error in your results for:

    i The weighing out of the calcium.

....

....

    ii The titrations.

....

....

....

....

    iii Systematic errors: calculate the total percentage errors in your measurements.

....

....

    iv Random errors: identify the random errors in the method.

....

....

f Are there any improvements you would make to this method?

....

....

Chapter outline

This chapter relates to Chapter 4: Chemical bonding and Chapter 5: States of matter in the coursebook.

In this chapter, you will complete investigations on:

- 2.1 Physical properties of three different types of chemical structure
- 2.2 Effect of temperature on the volume of a fixed mass of gas
- 2.3 Effect of pressure on the volume of a fixed mass of gas

Practical investigation 2.1:
Physical properties of three different types of chemical structure

Introduction

In this investigation, you will carry out some simple tests on substances that are examples of different types of chemical structure. You will then use your knowledge of the different chemical structural types to explain your observations.

Equipment

You will need:

- Bunsen burner, tripod, gauze and heatproof mat • 12 dry test tubes and a test-tube rack
- eight stoppers to fit test tubes • two graphite rods in a holder • three spatulas • three leads and two crocodile clips • 12 V bulb • power pack • wash bottle filled with distilled water • small evaporating basin • tongs

Access to:

- cyclohexane • wax • white sand • potassium iodide

Safety considerations

- Make sure you have read the advice in the Safety section at the beginning of this book and listen to any advice from your teacher before carrying out this investigation.

- You must wear eye protection at all times and tie back long hair.

- Cyclohexane is flammable and when using it you must turn off your Bunsen burner.

- Cyclohexane should be disposed of by pouring the mixture into a large glass bottle in the fume cupboard.

- If the test tube is very hot after heating, place it on the heatproof mat to allow it to cool.

Method

The three materials you are going to test are wax, silicon dioxide (sand) and potassium iodide.

Follow the methods explained in Table 2.1 and complete your observations as you proceed.

Test	Observations		
	Wax	Silicon dioxide	potassium iodide
1 Place a small sample of each material in a dry test tube and slowly increase the heat until it is very strong. Heat until there is no further change.			
2 Place a small amount of the substance in a dry test tube. Add some cyclohexane to the solid. Stopper the tube and shake it.			
3 Place a small amount of the substance in a dry test tube. Add some water to the solid. Stopper the tube and shake it.			
4 Place a small amount of the substance in an evaporating basin and test its electrical conductivity as a solid and then after the addition of the liquid in which it dissolved.			

Table 2.1

Summarise your findings in Table 2.2. Decide which of these three substances has a structure which is either giant covalent, simple molecular or giant ionic.

Substance	Type of chemical structure	Summary of observations

Table 2.2

Data analysis

a   Explain your observations for each of the **three** substances

   i   Wax

   ....

   ....

   ....

   ....

ii potassium iodide

....

....

....

....

iii Silicon dioxide

....

....

....

....

Practical investigation 2.2:
Effect of temperature on the volume of a fixed mass of gas

Introduction

In this investigation, you will determine how the volume of a fixed mass of gas varies with temperature at constant pressure.

Equipment

You will need:

- Bunsen burner, tripod, gauze and heatproof mat   • $100 \, cm^3$ round-bottomed flask
- stopper for flask attached to short length of plastic or rubber tubing   • $100 \, cm^3$ measuring cylinder   • permanent marker pen   • dropper   • $100 \, cm^3$ gas syringe
- metal container for heating water   • thermometer reading to $110 \, °C$ • either a stirring rod or a small 'paddle' for stirring water in metal container   • water supply

---

Safety considerations

- Long hair must be tied back securely.

- Eye protection must be worn at all times in this investigation.

- When you clamp the gas syringe do not over tighten the clamp as this could stop the piston from moving easily or even worse, break the glass.

- Do not use the thermometer for stirring. The thermometer bulb is only thin glass and is easily broken.

- When you stir the water in the metal container hold the container so that your stirring does not move it.

- Take special care when you are carrying out measurements at higher temperatures.

Method

1 In this first step you will determine the **true starting volume** of the gas. This needs to be done before the actual practical because the flask needs to be dry when doing the volume determinations. If this measurement is done the day before, the flask should be placed in an oven to dry it.

   • Insert the stopper into the neck of the round-bottomed flask and mark the level of the bottom of the stopper.

   • Pour water into the flask up to the mark.

   • Measure the volume of the water using the measuring cylinder.

   • Your teacher will give you the volume of the tubing.

   • What is the total volume of the flask and tubing?

   Total volume of the flask and tubing = ………. …… cm^3

2 Set up apparatus as shown in Figure 2.1.

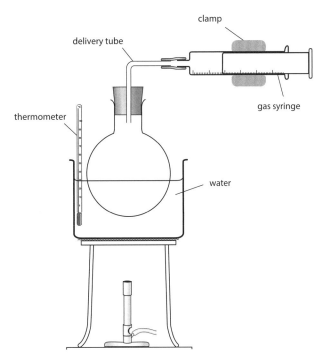

Figure 2.1

3 Measure the volume of the gas at room temperature.

4 Gently heat the water for a few seconds and at the same time stir the water thoroughly.

5 Remove the heat and measure the temperature.

6 Measure the volume of the gas in the syringe and add this to the volume of the flask and the tubing to give the total volume. If the temperature has risen too much then add some cold water to the container and stir again.

7 Repeat steps 5 and 6 until you have made measurements of the volume at several temperatures between room temperature and 90 °C.

8 Record your results in Table 2.3.

Temp/°C											
Reading on syringe/ml											
Total volume of gas/cm³											

Table 2.3

> **HINT**
> Your x-axis should start at −300 °C and end at 100 °C.

Data analysis

a Plot the temperature (horizontal axis) against total volume (vertical axis) on the graph paper provided.

- Plot a best-fit line through your points. You should omit any obviously anomalous points.

- Produce your line back to the value where the volume is **zero** and find the temperature at this point.

Temperature where volume is zero = …… …… °C

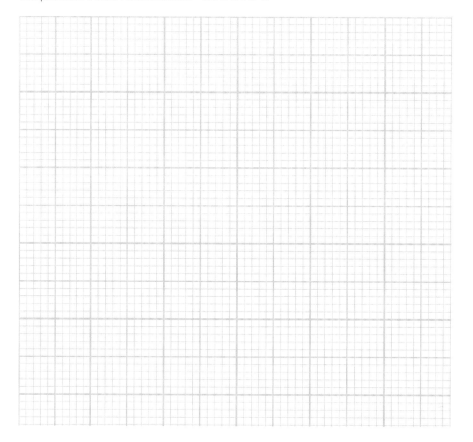

Evaluation

b Calculate the error in your answer for the absolute temperature. Look back at the Skills chapter for the formula, if required.

....

....

c Apart from the errors due to equipment, what were the other sources of error in your experiment?

……

……

d What is the name given to the temperature where the volume of the gas is zero?

……

e Using your results, write a law which can be applied to all gases and which defines the relationship between the volume and the temperature of an ideal gas.

……

……

Practical investigation 2.3:
Effect of pressure on the volume of a fixed mass of gas

Introduction

In this investigation, you will measure the pressure of a gas as its volume decreases and try to deduce the relationship between pressure and volume at constant temperature.

You will be using your pressure data logger to take readings at precise values of gas volume – this is described by some data logging systems as 'single-step mode'. If your software allows it you can export your results to Microsoft Excel for analysis.

Equipment

This experiment may be done as a demonstration by the teacher.

You will need:
• a 60 cm³ plastic syringe attached to a short length of plastic tubing that will fit the pressure data logger • a laptop or tablet that will interface with the data logger and run the software required • a pressure data logger with any software required

---

Safety considerations

* Eye protection must be worn at all times in this practical.
* Make sure your laptop is away from any water.
* Be careful that the tube connecting the pressure monitor to the syringe does not come off.

Method

1 Connect your syringe and pressure data logger. Each data logging system will have its own procedure for recording the separate values.

2 Starting at 60 cm³, measure the pressure of the gas at that volume.

HINT
At the lower volumes, the pressure will be relatively high, and someone will need to hold the syringe piston firmly while another records the pressure. Do not press down too forcefully on the piston!

3 Decrease the volume by pressing down the piston of the syringe and hold the piston at that point whilst the data logger records the pressure of the gas.

4 Measure the pressure at 5 cm³ intervals.

5 Record your results in Table 2.4.

Volume of gas/cm³	60	55	50	45	40	35	30	27
$\dfrac{1}{volume}$								
Pressure of gas/kPa								

Table 2.4

Data analysis

a From your results deduce the relationship between the **volume (V)** of a fixed mass of gas and its **pressure (P)**.

....

....

b Use a calculator or data processing package (e.g. Microsoft Excel) to calculate the values of $\dfrac{1}{V}$

c On the graph paper provided draw a graph of $\dfrac{1}{V}$ (horizontal axis) against P (vertical axis)

d Draw a best-fit line though the points.

e Explain why your graph shows that PV = constant.

....

....

....

f Take your first set of results.

Value of P = ...kPa; Value of V = ...m³; (Note 1 kPa = 1 x 10₃ Pa)

The universal gas equation states that $PV = nRT$;

P is in Pa; V is in m³ and $1 \text{ cm}^3 = 1 \times 10^{-6} \text{ m}^3$; n = number of moles of gas; T = absolute temperature (K). R is the Universal Gas Constant and its units are $J \, mol^{-1} \, K^{-1}$

If the initial volume = 60 cm³ then we can use the fact that n = $\dfrac{60}{24\,000}$ mol because this relationship is true at room temperature and pressure.

g Calculate the value of R by substituting your values into the ideal gas equation.

....

....

....

....

....

h Research the true value of R and calculate the percentage error in your result.

....

....

....

i Using the equation for R, explain why the units of $R = J \, mol^{-1} \, K^{-1}$

....

....

....

Chapter outline

This chapter relates to Chapter 6: Enthalpy changes in the coursebook.

In this chapter you will complete investigations on:

- 3.1 Enthalpy change for the reaction between zinc and aqueous copper(II) sulfate solution
- 3.2 Enthalpy change of combustion of alcohols
- 3.3 Enthalpy change of thermal decomposition
- 3.4 Change in enthalpy of hydration of copper (II) sulfate

Practical investigation 3.1:
Enthalpy change for the reaction between zinc and aqueous copper(II) sulfate

Introduction

In this practical, you will find the enthalpy change of reaction between zinc and copper(II) sulfate solution.

$$Zn(s) + CuSO_4(aq) \rightarrow ZnSO_4(aq) + Cu(s)$$

You will carry out the practical at least twice. The first experiment will have the zinc as the limiting reactant and the second will have the copper(II) sulfate as the limiting reactant. You can complete both of the practical investigations before answering the questions.

For both experiments you will construct a temperature–time graph. The reason for this is explained in the Skills chapter.

Equipment

You will need:

- two small polystyrene beakers • glass beaker large enough to hold the polystyrene beakers
- −10 to 110 °C thermometer • 25 cm³ measuring cylinder • plastic covers for polystyrene beakers • a small spatula • two weighing boats

Access to:

- 1 mol dm⁻³ copper(II) sulfate solution • zinc powder • a top-pan balance that reads to at least two decimal places

---

Safety considerations

- Make sure you have read the advice in the Safety section at the beginning of this book and listen to any advice from your teacher before carrying out this investigation.

- You must wear eye protection at all times.

- The zinc powder is flammable.

- Copper(II) sulfate solution is harmful to you and to the environment.

Part 1: Enthalpy change for the reaction with zinc as the limiting reactant.

Method

1   Measure out:

- 25.0 cm^3 of copper(II) sulfate solution into one of your polystyrene beakers. Place the polystyrene beaker into the glass beaker to support it.

- Between 0.64 g to 0.66 g of zinc powder.
  Mass of zinc powder = ………………..g

2   Measure the temperature of the copper(II) sulfate solution for the next three minutes. Swirl the solution regularly to make sure its temperature is uniform. Record your results in Table 3.1

3   On the third minute **do not measure the temperature**. Add the zinc powder to the copper(II) sulfate solution and for the next minute swirl the beaker so that the reactants are well mixed.

4   On the fourth minute resume the measurement of the temperature and continue measuring the temperature until the tenth minute. Record your results in Table 3.1

5   Between temperature measurements it is very important to swirl the beaker so that you have good mixing of the reactants and the solution.

Results

Time/min	0	1	2	3	4	5	6	7	8	9	10
Temperature/°C				X							

Table 3.1

Data analysis

a   What is the maximum temperature change (ΔT) in the first experiment?

……

The heat change (q) is calculated using the formula $q = m \times c \times \Delta T$ where m = mass of solution; c = specific heat capacity of solution and ΔT is the temperature change in the reaction

b   Calculate the enthalpy change for the reaction.

Assume that the density of the copper(II) sulfate solution is exactly the same as pure water (1.00 g cm^{-3}). Therefore, m = …………………….. g

The specific heat capacity of the solution is assumed to be the same as that of pure water. $c = 4.18\ Jg^{-1}K^{-1}$

………

………

………

25

c Calculate the number of moles of $CuSO_4$ present in 25.0 cm³ of 1.00 mol dm⁻³ solution.

....

....

d Calculate the number of moles of zinc present in your sample of zinc (A_r Zn = 65.4)

....

....

e Using the equation for the reaction and your answers to questions c and d above, explain why zinc is the limiting reactant in this experiment.

....

....

f Calculate the standard enthalpy change in kJ mol⁻¹

....

....

....

Part 2: Enthalpy change for the reaction with copper(II) sulfate as the limiting reactant.

Method

1 Measure out:

- 25.0 cm³ of copper(II) sulfate solution into one of your polystyrene beakers
- Between 6.40 g to 6.60 g of zinc powder

  Mass of zinc powder = ...g

2 Repeat Method Part 1, Steps 2–5 for the second mass of zinc and record your results in Table 3.2.

Results

Time/min	0	1	2	3	4	5	6	7	8	9	10
Temperature/°C				X							

Table 3.2

Data analysis

a Calculate the number of moles of copper(II) sulfate in 25.0 cm³ of 1.00 mol dm⁻³ solution. Number of moles of $CuSO_4$ = ... g

b Calculate the number of moles of zinc you weighed out. (A_r Zn) = 65.00 g.

c On the graph paper provided, plot the results of Part 1 and Part 2 of the investigation as follows:

- Plot a graph of temperature (vertical axis) against time (horizontal axis).
- Use the largest scale possible.
- For each experiment you should get two lines that look something like those shown in the Skills chapter.

d What is the maximum temperature change (ΔT) in the **second** experiment?

....

e Calculate the enthalpy change(q)for the reaction. Make the same assumptions you did for Part 1.

....

....

....

f Calculate the number of moles of $CuSO_4$ present in 25.0 cm³ of 1.00 mol dm⁻³ solution.

....

....

g Calculate the number of moles of zinc present in your sample of zinc
(A_r Zn = 65)

....

....

h Using the equation for the reaction and your answers to questions c and d above, explain why copper(II) sulfate is the limiting reactant in this experiment.

....

....

i Calculate the standard enthalpy change for the reaction in $kJ\,mol^{-1}$

....

....

....

j Explain why your two values should be either identical or very close in value.

....

....

Evaluation

k The accepted value for the enthalpy change of reaction is -219 $kJ\,mol^{-1}$. Calculate your percentage error using the average of your two results.

....

....

....

l Calculate the maximum percentage errors arising from your **mass**, **temperature** and **volume** measurements.

....

....

....

....

....

....

....

....

m Identify the sources of the **non**-systematic errors in your measurement.

....

....

....

Practical investigation 3.2:
Enthalpy change of combustion of alcohols

Introduction

Enthalpy change means the heat change at constant pressure.

In this practical you will investigate the enthalpy of combustion of the straight chain alcohols methanol, ethanol, propan-1-ol and butan-1-ol.

You will burn the alcohols using spirit burners. To make it a fair test you must make sure the enthalpy change measured is the same each time. Therefore, you will raise the temperature of a measured volume of water by the same temperature for each alcohol.

In this method, we are going to use a copper calorimeter as a container for the water being heated. When we heat up the water we are also heating up the calorimeter as well as the water.

The formula used for calculating heat change is $q = m \times c \times \Delta T$.

In this experiment:

Enthalpy change = $(m_{water} \times c_{water} \times \Delta T) + (m_{calorimeter} \times c_{calorimeter} \times \Delta T)$ J

The specific heat capacity for water = $4.18 \, J \, g^{-1} \, K^{-1}$

The specific heat capacity for copper = $0.385 \, J \, g^{-1} \, K^{-1}$

If you are using glass as a container then $c = 0.840 \, J \, g^{-1} \, K^{-1}$

HINT

m = mass;
c = specific heat capacity;
ΔT = change in temperature

Equipment

You will need:

• spirit burners containing the four alcohols • copper wire stirrer • clamp stand, boss and clamp • at least two heat-resistant pads • thermometer • 100 cm³ measuring cylinder • cap/cover for spirit burner • wooden splint

Access to:

• a top-pan balance reading to at least two decimal places • a supply of water • a Bunsen burner

---

Safety considerations

• Make sure you have read the advice in the Safety section at the beginning of this book and listen to any advice from your teacher before carrying out this investigation.

• You must wear eye protection at all times.

• All the alcohols are flammable.

• All the alcohols should be treated as harmful.

Method

Part 1: Preliminary planning

1   Weigh the copper calorimeter and stirrer.

2   Take a spirit burner containing methanol and position it where it will be placed in the actual experiment.

   a   Using a lighted splint, light the wick to get an idea of the height of the flame. The flame should be no more than 2 cm high.

   b   Clamp the calorimeter so that the flame just touches the base of the calorimeter (see Figure 3.1).

3   For meaningful measurements, the flame has to be the same for all four experiments and so has the distance between the flame and the base of the calorimeter. Extinguish the flame.

4   Add 100 cm³ of water to the calorimeter and see if the bulb of the thermometer is covered. If it isn't then you will need to increase the volume of water.

5   The experimental set-up should resemble that shown in Figure 3.1.

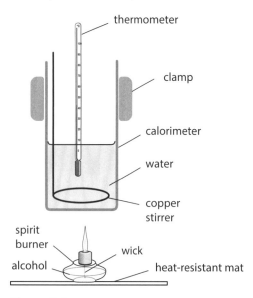

Figure 3.1

Part 2: Procedure

1   Measure out 100 cm³ of water into the calorimeter.

2   Make sure that the water covers the bulb of the thermometer. If it does not then the volume of water will have to be increased.

3   Clamp the calorimeter in the position and height that you decided upon in the preliminary planning.

4   Weigh the spirit burner plus the cap/cover if one is available.

   Mass of burner + methanol = ………………….…g

5   Stir the water thoroughly and measure its temperature.

   Initial temperature of water = …………………..°C

6 a Remove the cap from the burner and place it underneath the calorimeter.

  b Light the wick using a lighted splint.

7 Stir the water thoroughly until the temperature has risen by exactly 20 °C.

Final temperature of water   ……………………..°C

8 a Blow out the flame and cover with the cap/cover if one is provided.

  b Carry the burner over to the top-pan balance using a heat-resistant pad and weigh it.

Mass of burner + methanol = …………………..g

Mass of methanol burned = …………………..g

9 Repeat Steps 1–8 using the other three alcohols and record your results in Table 3.3

Methanol	Mass of burner + methanol before burning		g
	Mass of burner + methanol after burning		g
	Mass of **methanol** burned		g
Ethanol	Mass of burner + ethanol before burning		g
	Mass of burner + ethanol after burning		g
	Mass of **ethanol** burned		g
Propan-1-ol	Mass of burner + propan-1-ol before burning		g
	Mass of burner + propan-1-ol after burning		g
	Mass of **propan**-1-ol burned		g
Butan-1-ol	Mass of burner + butan-1-ol before burning		g
	Mass of burner + butan-1-ol after burning		g
	Mass of **butan-1-ol** burned		g

Table 3.3

Data analysis

The enthalpy change is the same for all four alcohols because you heated up the same mass of water and the same apparatus by the same temperature. Remember this value is in J and standard enthalpy changes are usually expressed in kJ.

If the mass of methanol burned is m g then the number of moles of methanol (n) burned in the experiment

$$= \frac{m}{Mr} = \frac{m}{32}$$

If the enthalpy change is q then the standard enthalpy change of combustion (ΔH_c) can be calculated as follows: $\Delta H_c = \frac{q}{n} \div 1000 \text{ kJ mol}^{-1}$

a Calculate the standard enthalpy changes of combustion for all four alcohols and record your results in Table 3.4.

Name of alcohol	Relative molecular mass	No. of moles burned/mol	Experimental value for ΔH_c /kJ mol^{-1}	Literature value for ΔH_c/ kJ mol^{-1}
Methanol(CH$_3$OH)				−726
Ethanol (C$_2$H$_5$OH)				−1367
Propan-1-ol (C$_3$H$_7$OH)				−2021
Butan-1-ol (C$_4$H$_9$OH)				−2676

Table 3.4

b Calculate the percentage error in your results for each alcohol.

i Methanol

....

....

ii Ethanol

....

....

iii Propan-1-ol

....

....

....

iv Butan-1-ol

....

....

....

c What was the maximum percentage error from your apparatus?

....

....

i The measurement of temperature (note for each temperature change there were two readings taken)

....

....

    ii The measurement of the water volume

....

....

d The measurement of mass of alcohol burned for each alcohol:

    i Methanol

....

....

    ii Ethanol

....

....

    iii Propan-1-ol

....

....

    iv Butan-1-ol

....

....

e Choose **one** alcohol and calculate the maximum percentage error due to the apparatus used.

....

....

....

f What other sources of error could lead to inaccuracies in your results?

....

....

....

....

....

Practical investigation 3.3:
Enthalpy change of thermal decomposition

Introduction

When potassium hydrogen carbonate is heated it decomposes into potassium carbonate, carbon dioxide and water.

$$2KHCO_3(s) \rightarrow K_2CO_3(s) + CO_2(g) + H_2O(l)$$

Because this is a thermal decomposition and is an endothermic reaction, it is impossible to find the enthalpy change directly. To overcome this problem we use Hess' Law to find the enthalpy change indirectly.

Both potassium hydrogen carbonate and potassium carbonate react with hydrochloric acid and the enthalpy changes are measurable.

$$KHCO_3(s) + HCl(aq) \rightarrow KCl(aq) + H_2O(l) + CO_2(g) \qquad \text{Enthalpy change} = \Delta H_1$$

$$K_2CO_3(s) + 2HCl(aq) \rightarrow 2KCl(aq) + H_2O(l) + CO_2(g) \qquad \text{Enthalpy change} = \Delta H_2$$

We can construct a Hess' cycle for this reaction (see Figure 3.2)

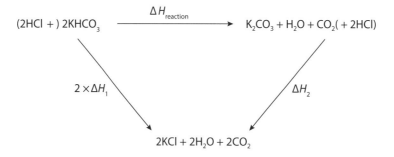

Figure 3.2

Using Hess' Law $\Delta H_r + \Delta H_2 = 2\Delta H_1$

Therefore, $\Delta H_r = 2\Delta H_1 - \Delta H_2$ and by determining the values of ΔH_1 and ΔH_2 we will be able to calculate the enthalpy change for the reaction.

Equipment

You will need:

• polystyrene beaker and cap with hole for thermometer • glass beaker to hold the polystyrene beaker • thermometer: one reading from −10 to 50 °C with 0.2 °C divisions is preferable • weighing boat • 50 cm³ measuring cylinder • cotton wool to act as extra insulation

Access to:

• potassium carbonate solid • potassium hydrogen carbonate solid • 2 mol dm⁻³ hydrochloric acid • a top-pan balance reading to at least two decimal places

---

Safety considerations

• Make sure you have read the advice in the Safety section at the beginning of this book and listen to any advice from your teacher before carrying out this investigation.

• Wear eye protection at all times.

• The hydrochloric acid is an irritant at this concentration.

Method

Part 1: Determining the enthalpy change for Reaction 1.

1 Weigh out 0.025 mol of potassium hydrogen carbonate.

 [Ar values: K = 39.1; H = 1; C = 12; O = 16]

2 Formula mass of potassium hydrogen carbonate = ...g mol⁻¹

3 Mass of 0.025 mol = ...g

4 Mass of potassium hydrogen carbonate weighed out = ...g

5 **a** Place the polystyrene beaker inside the glass beaker and fit the cotton wool round it to improve the insulation (as shown in Figure 3.3).

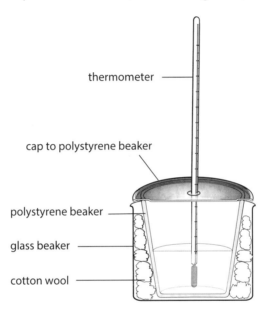

thermometer

cap to polystyrene beaker

polystyrene beaker

glass beaker

cotton wool

Figure 3.3

 b Measure 50.0 cm³ of 2.00 mol dm⁻³ hydrochloric acid and pour it into the polystyrene beaker.

6 Measure the initial temperature of the acid.

 Initial temperature of acid = ...°C

7 Add the potassium hydrogen carbonate to the acid. There will be a rapid effervescence so make sure you have the cap ready to prevent any spillages.

8 Swirl the beaker and contents to ensure that there is thorough mixing of the contents.

9 When the reaction is complete, record the minimum temperature.

 Final temperature of the Reaction 1 mixture = ...°C

Part 2: Determining the enthalpy change for Reaction 2.

1 Weigh out 0.025 mol of potassium carbonate.

 [Ar values: K = 39.1; C = 12; O = 16]

2 Formula mass of potassium carbonate = ...g mol⁻¹

3 Mass of 0.025 mol = ...g

4 Mass of potassium carbonate weighed out = ...g

5   Place the polystyrene beaker inside the glass beaker and fit the cotton wool round it to improve the insulation

6   Measure 50 cm³ of 2 mol dm⁻³ hydrochloric acid and pour it into the polystyrene beaker.

7   Measure the initial temperature of the acid.

Initial temperature of acid = ...°C

8   a   Add the potassium carbonate to the acid. Once again there will be a rapid effervescence so make sure you have the cap ready to prevent any spillages.

    b   Swirl the beaker and contents to ensure that there is thorough mixing of the contents.

9   When the reaction is complete, record the maximum temperature attained.

Final temperature of the Reaction 2 mixture = ...°C

Data analysis

a   Complete Table 3.5

Temperature	Reaction 1	Reaction 2
Final temperature/°C		
Initial temperature/°C		
Temperature change (ΔT)/°C		

Table 3.5

The enthalpy change for each reaction (q) = m x specific heat capacity x ΔT

Assume the density of the hydrochloric acid is 1.00 g dm⁻³ and its specific heat capacity is 4.18 J g⁻¹ K⁻¹.

b   Calculate the value of q for Reaction 1

....

....

....

c   Calculate the enthalpy change of reaction for Reaction 1

....

....

....

d   Calculate the value of q for Reaction 2

....

....

....

e Calculate the enthalpy change of reaction for Reaction 2

....

....

....

f Use these two results to find the enthalpy change for the thermal decomposition of potassium hydrogen carbonate.

Evaluation

The standard enthalpies of formation (in kJ mol^{-1}), relevant to this reaction is follows:

$\Delta H_f^{\ominus}(KHCO_3)= -959.4$; $\Delta H_f^{\ominus}(K_2CO_3)=-1146$; $\Delta H_f^{\ominus}(CO_2)=-393.5$; $\Delta H_f^{\ominus}(H_2O) = -285.9$

g Using these values calculate the standard enthalpy change for the reaction.

....

....

....

h Calculate the percentage error in your results.

....

....

....

i Calculate the maximum percentage error due to the apparatus used.

....

....

....

....

....

....

....

....

Practical investigation 3.4:
Change in enthalpy of hydration of copper (II) sulfate

Introduction

This practical brings together techniques and theory used in previous investigations. The reaction being studied is as follows:

$$CuSO_4 (s) + 5H_2O(l) \rightarrow CuSO_4. 5H_2O(s)$$

It is impossible to determine the enthalpy change of this reaction directly. Therefore, we have to use Hess's law. Hess's cycle is shown in Figure 3.4.

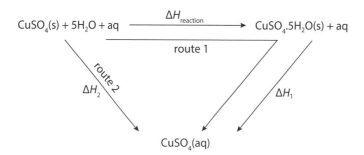

Figure 3.4

Using the cycle, you can see that the arrows meet at $CuSO_4(aq)$ (i.e. an aqueous solution of copper(II) sulfate). However, to get to this solution, the enthalpy change must be the same.

This means that: $\Delta H_{reaction} + \Delta H_1 = \Delta H_2$

In one of the reactions, the temperature change is reasonably high and for this reason you are going to collect results for a temperature–time graph.

Equipment

You will need:

• two polystyrene beakers plus caps • thermometer which reads from -10 °C to 50 °C in 0.2 °C divisions • spatula • wash bottle containing distilled water • glass beaker large enough to hold the polystyrene beakers • cotton wool to improve the insulation of the polystyrene beakers • a 50 cm³ measuring cylinder • weighing boats x 2

Access to:

• a top-pan balance which reads at least to two decimal places • anhydrous copper(II) sulfate • hydrated copper(II) sulfate crystals • distilled water • paper towels

---

Safety considerations

- Make sure you have read the advice in the Safety section at the beginning of this book and listen to any advice from your teacher before carrying out this investigation.

- Eye protection must be worn at all times during this experiment.

- The copper(II) sulfate solution is an irritant and copper(II) sulfate is harmful to the environment; any solution should be poured into a bottle and re-used.

Part 1: Determination of ΔH_2

Method

1   Weigh out 0.025 moles of anhydrous copper(II) sulfate.

(Relative atomic masses: Cu = 63.5; S = 32.1 and O = 16)

Relative formula mass of copper(II) sulfate = ...g mol^{-1}

Mass of anhydrous copper(II) sulfate = ...g

Therefore, number of moles of anhydrous copper(II) sulfate = ...mol

2   Measure out 50 cm^3 of distilled water into one of the polystyrene beakers. Place the polystyrene beaker into the glass beaker and surround it with cotton wool to improve insulation.

3   **a**   Measure the temperature of the distilled water every minute for the next three minutes.

    b   Record your measurements in the Table 3.6.

4   On the fourth minute do not measure the temperature but add the anhydrous copper(II) sulfate to the distilled water and for the next minute swirl the glass beaker and polystyrene beaker vigorously in order to help the dissolving of the anhydrous copper(II) sulfate.

5   On the fifth minute continue with the measurement of the temperature and do so every minute until ten minutes has elapsed.

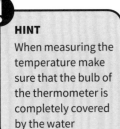

HINT

When measuring the temperature make sure that the bulb of the thermometer is completely covered by the water

Results

Time/min	0	1	2	3	4	5	6	7	8	9	10
Temperature/°C					X						

Table 3.6

Data analysis

a   Draw a graph of time (horizontal axis) against temperature (vertical axis) for the determination of ΔH_2.

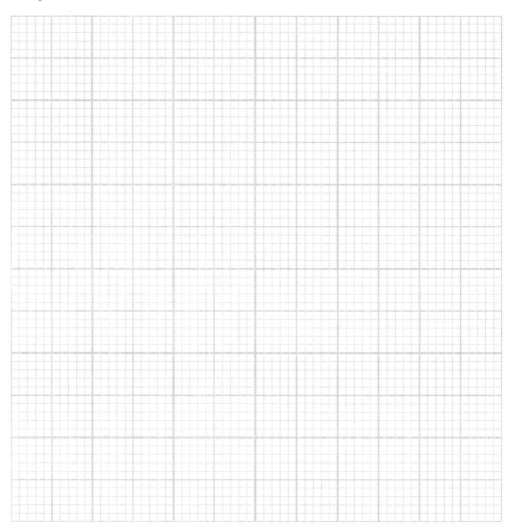

b   From your graph determine the initial and final temperatures.

Initial temperature = ...°C; final temperature =............................°C

c   Temperature change = ...°C

d   Enthalpy change for _____mol = ... J

e   Therefore, standard enthalpy change of reaction (ΔH_2) = ...kJ mol^{-1}

Part 2: Determination of ΔH_1

Method

1   Weigh out 0.025 moles of $CuSO_4.5H_2O$ crystals.

(Relative atomic masses: Cu = 63.5; S = 32.1 and O = 16)

Record:

a Relative formula mass of $CuSO_4.5H_2O$ crystals = ...g mol^{-1}

b Mass of $CuSO_4.5H_2O$ crystals = ...g

c Therefore number of moles of $CuSO_4.5H_2O$ crystals = ...mol

This mass of $CuSO_4.5H_2O$ crystals already contains some water because of the water of crystallisation and this has to be taken into consideration when measuring out the water in which the copper(II) sulfate crystals are to be dissolved.

For example, if you weigh out 0.0250 mol of $CuSO_4.5H_2O$ then the number of moles of water = 5 x 0.0250 = 0.125 mol and the mass of water present = 0.125 x 18 g = 2.25 g. Therefore, you weigh out 50 – 2.25 g of water = 47.75 g

d Number of moles of water in _____mol of copper(II) sulfate crystals = ... mol

e Mass of water present in the crystals = ...g

Therefore, this mass of water (m) has to be subtracted from the mass of water we will measure out for the 2nd enthalpy determination.

f Mass of water to be weighed out = ...g of water

2 a Take the other polystyrene beaker and place it on the top-pan balance.

b Zero (Tare) the balance and weigh out ....g of water.

3 Replace the polystyrene beaker from the previous experiment with the new one in the glass beaker.

4 Wash the thermometer thoroughly with distilled water and wipe dry with a paper towel.

5 Add the 0.025 mol of copper(II) sulfate crystals to the distilled water.

6 Swirl the glass and polystyrene beakers until all the copper sulfate has dissolved.

7 Measure the following temperatures obtained for this solution:

a Minimum temperature = ...°C

b Initial temperature = ...°C

c Final temperature =........................°C

Data analysis

a Calculate the temperature change = ...°C

b Calculate enthalpy change for _____mol = ... J

= ....mol

c Calculate the standard enthalpy change of reaction (ΔH_2) = ...kJ mol^{-1}

d Calculate the enthalpy change for the following chemical change:

$CuSO_4 (s) + 5H_2O(l) \rightarrow CuSO_4. 5H_2O(s)$

....

....

....

....

Evaluation

The accepted value for the enthalpy change is = −78.2 kJ mol^{-1}

e Calculate the percentage error in your experiment.

....

....

....

f Calculate the maximum expected percentage errors from your all your items of apparatus and account for the percentage error in your experiment.

....

....

....

....

....

Chapter outline

This chapter refers to Chapter 7: The properties of metals in the coursebook

In this chapter you will complete investigations on:

- 4.1 Understanding redox (I): investigating a reactivity series and displacement reactions
- 4.2 Understanding redox (II): investigating further reactions

Practical investigation 4.1:

Understanding redox (I): investigating reactivity series and displacement reactions

Introduction

You have already studied displacement reactions involving metals and metal salts. See Figure 4.1 for a reminder of the effects of adding sodium hydroxide to a) solution of iron(II) ions b) solution of iron(III) ions and c) solution of zinc ions. Initially, you will note there is a white precipitate of zinc hydroxide and then when excess sodium hydroxide is added the precipitate dissolves.

In this investigation you will take these studies further by identifying the products and explaining the redox nature of the reactions using oxidation numbers. You will use ionic equations to represent the reactions and to clarify what is actually happening in these reactions.

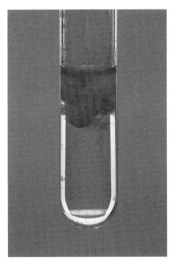  

Figure 4.1

Equipment

You will need:

• 10 test tubes • two test-tube racks • six droppers • wooden splint • Bunsen burner and heatproof mat • small spatula • small glass filter funnel and three filter papers

Access to:

• 0.500 mol dm⁻³ copper(II) nitrate solution • 0.500 mol dm⁻³ zinc nitrate solution
• 2.00 mol dm⁻³ hydrochloric acid • 2.00 mol dm⁻³ sodium hydroxide solution
• magnesium ribbon • magnesium powder • iron powder • zinc powder

Safety considerations

- Make sure you have read the advice in the Safety section at the beginning of this book and listen to any advice from your teacher before carrying out this investigation.

- You must wear eye protection at all times.

- The metal powders and the magnesium ribbon are flammable and must be kept away from naked flames.

- The hydrochloric acid is an irritant at this concentration.

- The copper(II) nitrate is harmful and is an environmental hazard.

- The sodium hydroxide solution is corrosive.

Method

There are a number of reactions to investigate, which are summarised in Table 4.1

Reaction number	Reactants	Instructions
1	Magnesium and hydrochloric acid	• To a 1 cm depth of hydrochloric acid in a test tube, add a 1 cm length of magnesium ribbon. • Collect any gas evolved and test with a lighted splint. • Add sodium hydroxide solution to the solution formed by the reaction.
2	Iron and copper(II) nitrate solution	• To a 1 cm depth of copper(II) nitrate solution in a test tube, add one full spatula of iron powder. • When the reaction is complete, filter the resulting mixture. • Test the filtrate by adding sodium hydroxide solution drop by drop.
3	Zinc and copper(II) nitrate solution	• To a 1 cm depth of copper(II) nitrate solution in a test tube, add one full spatula of zinc powder. • When the reaction is complete, filter the resulting mixture. • Test the filtrate by adding sodium hydroxide solution drop by drop.
4	Magnesium and zinc nitrate	• To a 1 cm depth of zinc nitrate solution in a test tube, add one full spatula of magnesium powder. • When the reaction is complete, filter the resulting mixture. • Test the filtrate by adding sodium hydroxide solution drop by drop.

Table 4.1

Results

For each reaction mixture, note down your observations in Table 4.2.

Reaction number	Observations
1	
2	
3	
4	

Table 4.2

Data analysis and evaluation

For each Reaction **1–4** (Table 4.1):

a Give the names of the products of the reaction and justify your answer by referring to your observations.

b Write the ionic equation for the reaction taking place and for any test that has been used.

c Explain why the reaction is a redox reaction.

Reaction 1

a ....

....

....

b ....

....

c ....

....

....

Reaction 2

a ....

....

....

b ....

....

c ....

....

....

Reaction 3

a ....

....

....

b ....

....

c ....

....

....

Reaction 4

a ....

....

....

b ....

....

c ....

....

....

Practical investigation 4.2:
Understanding redox (II): investigating further reactions

Introduction

In this investigation you will look at further redox reactions and gain confidence in recognising when reactants have been reduced or oxidised.

Equipment

You will need:

- 10 test tubes • two test-tube racks • six droppers (graduated if possible)
- plastic gloves • small spatula

Access to:

- $0.0200\,mol\,dm^{-3}$ potassium manganate(VII) solution • $0.100\,mol\,dm^{-3}$ iron(II) sulfate solution • $2.00\,mol\,dm^{-3}$ sodium hydroxide solution • '20 volume' hydrogen peroxide solution • $1.00\,mol\,dm^{-3}$ sulfuric acid • $0.100\,mol\,dm^{-3}$ sodium sulfite (sodium sulfate(IV)) solution • $0.100\,mol\,dm^{-3}$ iron(III) sulfate solution • $0.100\,mol\,dm^{-3}$ barium chloride solution • $0.100\,mol\,dm^{-3}$ sodium sulfate (sodium sulfate(VI)) solution • $2.00\,mol\,dm^{-3}$ hydrochloric acid • 1:1 hydrochloric acid (solution of equal volumes of concentrated hydrochloric acid and distilled water)

Safety considerations

- Make sure you have read the advice in the Safety section at the beginning of this book and listen to any advice from your teacher before carrying out this investigation.
- Wear eye protection at all times.
- The potassium manganate(VII) solution is harmful and can cause brown stains on skin and clothing – if possible wear plastic gloves.
- '20 volume' hydrogen peroxide solution is an irritant and can cause white stains on skin.
- The concentrated hydrochloric acid is corrosive.

Method

As with Practical investigation 4.1, there are a number of experiments and the details are summarised in Table 4.3

Reaction number	Reactants	Instructions
1	Fe^{2+}(aq) and acidified MnO_4^-(aq)	<ul><li>Add the iron(II) sulfate to a depth of 1 cm in a test tube. Add five drops of sulfuric acid and then add five drops of the solution of potassium manganate(VII).</li><li>Add sodium hydroxide solution to the resulting solution.</li></ul>
2	H_2O_2 and SO_3^{2-}(aq)	<ul><li>Add 1 cm³ of sodium sulfate solution to a test tube. Add three drops of barium chloride solution. To the resulting mixture, add hydrochloric acid drop by drop until there is no further change.</li><li>Add 1 cm³ of sodium sulfite solution to a test tube. Add three drops of barium chloride solution. To the resulting mixture, add hydrochloric acid drop by drop until there is no further change.</li><li>To 1 cm³ of sodium sulfite solution in a test tube, add an equal volume of hydrogen peroxide solution. Add barium chloride solution. Then add dilute hydrochloric acid.</li></ul>
3	Concentrated HCl and iron; addition of hydrogen peroxide solution to the product.	<ul><li>Add 1:1 hydrochloric acid to a test tube to a depth of 2 cm.</li><li>Add a small spatula of iron powder. Mix thoroughly.</li><li>Allow the reaction to proceed for a few minutes. Make and record your observations.</li><li>Split the resulting solution into two separate portions in two clean test tubes.</li><li>To one of the two portions add sodium hydroxide solution until in excess.</li><li>To the other portion add a few drops of hydrogen peroxide solution.</li><li>Then add sodium hydroxide solution to the second portion.</li></ul>

Table 4.3

Results

For each reaction mixture note your observations in Table 4.4. You need to complete the headings for the table yourself.

	....
	....
	....

Table 4.4

Data analysis and evaluation

Reaction 1

a   For the reaction between **iron(II) ions** and **manganate(VII) ions** explain how your
   observations show that a reaction has occurred.

   ....

   The half-equation for the reduction of the manganate(VII) is

   $$MnO_4^-(aq) + 8H^+(aq) + 5e^- \rightarrow Mn^{2+}(aq) + 4H_2O(aq).$$

b   Explain why this is reduction.

   ....

c   Write a half-equation for the oxidation of the $Fe^{2+}(aq)$ ions.

   ....

d   Write the balanced ionic equation for the reaction and using oxidation numbers explain why the
   reaction between iron(II) and manganate(VII) ions is a redox reaction.

   ....

   ....

   ....

   ....

Reaction 2

e   Using your observations explain how you can distinguish sulfite ions (SO_3^{2-}) from sulfate
   ions(SO_4^{2-}). Give **three** balanced ionic equations, including state symbols for the reactions
   taking place.

   ....

   ....

   ....

   ....

   ....

f   What are the products of the reaction between sulfite ions and hydrogen peroxide? Explain your
   answer and write the balanced ionic equations for the reactions taking place.

   ....

   ....

   ....

   ....

g Explain why this is a redox reaction.

……

……

……

Reaction 3a – the reaction between iron and hydrochloric acid.

h Explain your observations of the reaction between the iron and hydrochloric acid. You need to give the final oxidation number of the iron in the iron compound formed and provide evidence for your answer.

……

……

……

i Explain why this is a redox reaction.

……

……

……

Reaction 3b – the reaction between the product of Reaction 3a and hydrogen peroxide.

j Explain your observations and give the balanced ionic equation for the reaction.

……

……

……

……

k Explain why this reaction is a redox reaction.

……

……

……

Chapter 5:
Chemical equilibrium

Chapter outline

This chapter refers to Chapter 8: Equilibrium in the coursebook.

In this chapter you will complete investigations on:

- 5.1 Applying Le Chatelier's principle to a gaseous equilibrium
- 5.2 Applying Le Chatelier's principle to an aqueous equilibrium
- 5.3 The equilibrium constant for the hydrolysis of ethyl ethanoate.

Practical investigation 5.1:
Applying Le Chatelier's principle to a gaseous equilibrium

Introduction

In this investigation, you will apply Le Chatelier's principle to the gaseous equilibrium shown below:

$$2NO_2(g) \rightleftharpoons N_2O_4(g)$$

Equipment

You will need:

- a 250 cm³ beaker and a 100 cm³ beaker • some mouldable putty / modelling clay to block the end of a tube • a plastic dropper with the narrow stem removed • plastic gloves • one piece of plain white paper as a background for viewing changes • a Bunsen burner tripod and gauze (if a kettle is not available)

Access to:

- ice • hot water from either a kettle or by heating water yourself • copper turnings
- concentrated nitric acid

Safety considerations:

- Make sure you have read the advice in the Safety section at the beginning of this book and listen to any advice from your teacher before carrying out this investigation.

- Nitrogen dioxide is a toxic gas and all the operations involving it before it is in the sealed dropper **must** be done in a fume cupboard.

- Concentrated nitric acid is corrosive and will give yellow stains on skin. Wear plastic gloves when dealing with the acid.

- Take care when using the hot water.

Method

Part 1: Preparing a dropper of nitrogen dioxide gas

All the preparation must be done in a fume cupboard. You will also need to wear gloves for the preparation.

1 Add some copper turnings to a 100 cm³ beaker placed in a fume cupboard.

2 Add a few cm³ of concentrated nitric acid to the copper.

3 Quickly expel the air from the dropper and then suck up the brown nitrogen dioxide gas from above the reaction mixture in the beaker.

4 When you can see that the dropper is full of brown gas, seal the opening to the dropper using mouldable putty and make sure that it is well sealed.

Part 2: Investigating the equilibrium

1 a Place some ice in a 250 cm³ beaker ¼ full of water and leave for a few minutes.

   b Take your dropper of gas and hold the bulb in the cold water. Make observations about any changes in the appearance of the gas in the bulb. Record your results in Table 5.1.

2 a Empty the cold water from the beaker and replace it with hot water.

   b Note the colour and intensity of the gas in the bulb and then place it gently in the hot water. Note any changes that occur.

3 a Whilst you are holding the mouldable putty firmly in place, squeeze the bulb of the dropper. Note any changes in the appearance of the gas.

   b Release the pressure on the bulb and again note any changes in the appearance of the gas.

Results

Record your observations in Table 5.1.

Conditions		Observations
Effect of changing temperature	Increase	
	Decrease	
Effect of changing pressure	Increase	

Table 5.1

Evaluation

The equation for the equilibrium is: $2NO_2 \rightleftharpoons N_2O_4$

brown gas   colourless gas

a Describe what happens to the amount of nitrogen dioxide present in the equilibrium mixture when the temperature is:

   i Decreased

ii Increased

....

....

iii What do your results tell you about the thermochemical nature (exothermic or endothermic) of the forward and backward reactions? Refer to Le Chatelier's principle in your answer.

....

....

....

....

....

b Describe what happens to the amount of nitrogen dioxide present in the equilibrium mixture when the pressure is increased and explain these changes using Le Chatelier's principle.

....

....

....

....

Practical investigation 5.2:
Applying Le Chatelier's principle to an aqueous equilibrium

Introduction

In this investigation, you will apply Le Chatelier's principle to the aqueous equilibrium shown below:

$$[Cu(H_2O)_6]^{2+}(aq) + 4Cl^-(aq) \rightleftharpoons [CuCl_4]^{2-}(aq) + 6H_2O(l)$$

blue   yellow

Equipment

You will need:

• one dropper   • 10 test tubes   • test-tube rack that can accommodate at least two boiling tubes   • two boiling tubes   • one boiling tube rubber bung   • 100 cm³ beaker for distilled water   • permanent marker pen   • wash bottle filled with distilled water • three 250 cm³ beakers   • one sheet of plain white paper to act as a background

Access to:

• concentrated hydrochloric acid   • 1 mol dm⁻³ aqueous copper(ii) sulfate solution • distilled water   • ice

Safety considerations

- Make sure you have read the advice in the Safety section at the beginning of this book and listen to any advice from your teacher before carrying out this investigation.
- Eye protection must be worn at all times during the investigation.
- Concentrated hydrochloric acid is corrosive.
- Copper(II) sulfate is harmful and is an environmental hazard.

Part 1 – Effect of concentration changes on the position of equilibrium

Method

1. Half-fill one of the boiling tubes with concentrated hydrochloric acid (CARE!) and place a bung in the neck to stop fumes escaping into the laboratory.

2. Half-fill the other boiling tube with aqueous copper(II) sulfate solution.

3. Place the 10 test tubes in the test-tube rack and number them 1 to 10.

4. Take your dropper and use it to add copper(II) sulfate solution to each of the test tubes as shown in Table 5.2.

Tube number	1	2	3	4	5	6	7	8	9	10
No. drops of Cu^{2+}(aq)	10	9	8	7	6	5	4	3	2	1

Table 5.2

5. Wash your dropper thoroughly with distilled water and then rinse with concentrated hydrochloric acid.

6. Carefully add concentrated hydrochloric acid to the test tubes as shown in Table 5.3.

Tube number	1	2	3	4	5	6	7	8	9	10
No. drops of copper(II) sulfate	10	9	8	7	6	5	4	3	2	1
No. drops of conc. HCl	0	1	2	3	4	5	6	7	8	9

Table 5.3

Results

Write down the trend in colour as the concentration of hydrochloric acid (Cl⁻ ions) is increased.

....

....

....

Evaluation

a Explain the change in colour as the concentration of Cl^- is increased – refer to Le Chatelier's principle in your explanation.

....

....

....

....

Part 2 – Effect of temperature on the position of equilibrium

Method

1 Make up three samples of mixture 6 (5 drops : 5 drops) in three different test tubes.

2 Add some ice to a small amount of water in the $250\,cm^3$ beaker.

3 Take one of the test tubes containing the equilibrium mixture and place it in the ice–water mixture. Allow a few minutes for any changes to occur and compare with the control tube. Record your observations in Table 5.4.

4 In the second beaker place some water at room temperature. Place another of the test tubes in the water and leave for a few minutes. **This is the control experiment**.

5 In the final beaker add some boiling water. (CARE!) Place the third test tube in the beaker of boiling water. Leave for a few minutes and then compare it with the control. Record your observations in Table 5.4.

Results

Conditions	Observations
0 °C	....
Room temperature	**Control**
Boiling water	....

Table 5.4

Evaluation

b Describe what happens to the amount of $[CuCl_4]^{2-}$(aq) present in the equilibrium mixture when the temperature is:

i Decreased

....

ii Increased

....

c What do your results tell you about the thermochemical nature (exothermic or endothermic) of the forward and backward reactions? Refer to Le Chatelier's principle in your answer.

....

....

....

....

Practical investigation 5.3:
The equilibrium constant for the hydrolysis of ethyl ethanoate

Introduction

In this investigation you will determine the equilibrium constant, K_c, for the following reaction:

$$CH_3COOC_2H_5(l) + H_2O(l) \xrightleftharpoons[]{H^{+(aq)} \text{ catalyst}} CH_3COOH(l) + C_2H_5OH(l)$$

Equipment

You will need:

- 500 cm³ volumetric flask • thymolphthalein indicator • 250 cm³ conical flask
- white tile • small filter funnel for filling burette • six sample tubes • container for sample tubes or rubber band to keep them together • permanent marker pen
- 50.00 cm³ burette • two 5.00 cm³ or 10.00 cm³ graduated pipettes • wash bottle containing distilled water

Access to:

- ethyl ethanoate • 2.00 mol dm⁻³ hydrochloric acid • 1.00 mol dm⁻³ sodium hydroxide solution

---

Safety considerations

- Make sure you have read the advice in the Safety section at the beginning of this book and listen to any advice from your teacher before carrying out this investigation.

- You must wear eye protection at all times.

- Ethyl ethanoate is flammable and the vapour is harmful.

- The hydrochloric acid is an irritant at this concentration and the sodium hydroxide is corrosive.

Method

Part 1: Setting up the reaction mixtures

This first part involves setting up the reaction mixtures with different amounts of ethyl ethanoate and water.

1 Take your six sample tubes and number them 1 to 6 using your permanent marker pen.

2 For each sample tube, set up the mixtures as shown in Table 5.5.

Tube number	Volume of hydrochloric acid/cm³	Volume of ethyl ethanoate/cm³	Volume of water/cm³
1	5	0	5
2	5	1	4
3	5	2	3
4	5	3	2
5	5	4	1
6	5	5	0

Table 5.5

3 Make sure the contents of each tube are thoroughly mixed but **do not shake too vigorously**. You do not want the more volatile contents to escape.

4 Leave the tubes in a place that will be at room temperature for most of the time. Remember: you will leave at least two days for the mixture to come to equilibrium. Over the intervening time make sure that the tubes are well shaken. You will notice that the two separate layers present at the beginning merge into one layer.

Part 2: Analysis of the reaction to determine the composition of the equilibrium mixture

1 Rinse the burette with the $1.00 \, mol \, dm^{-3}$ sodium hydroxide solution and then fill it with the alkaline solution. Use the Skills Chapter, if necessary, to remind yourself how to do this.

2 a Add the contents of Tube 1 to a $250 \, cm^3$ conical flask.

  b Wash the tube several times until you cannot smell any residual ester or ethanoic acid in the tube.

  c Place the flask on a white tile under the burette tap and add a few drops of thymolphthalein indicator.

3 Before you do your titration you should have an estimate of the volume of the $1.00 \, mol \, dm^{-3}$ sodium hydroxide solution you will need to neutralise the hydrochloric acid present in the sample tube.

  Number of moles of hydrochloric acid present = ……………… mol

  The equation for the neutralisation of the acid by the sodium hydroxide is:

  $$NaOH(aq) + HCl(aq) \longrightarrow NaCl(aq) + H_2O(l)$$

  Therefore, the number of moles of sodium hydroxide required = ……………mol

  This means that the estimated volume of sodium hydroxide required $= \dfrac{n}{C} =$ ………cm^3

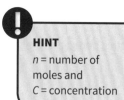

HINT

n = number of moles and
C = concentration

4 Using the value of your estimated volume, you can safely run in $2 \, cm^3$ less than this value before you start adding the alkali drop by drop.

5 When the indicator changes from colourless to blue, stop adding the alkali and record the burette reading in Table 5.6.

6 Wash out your conical flask. Repeat Steps 2–5 with Tubes 2–6 and record your results in Table 5.6.

Results

Tube number	1	2	3	4	5	6
Final burette reading/cm³						
Initial burette reading/cm³						
Titre /cm³						

Table 5.6

Data analysis

a Explain what the titration results tell you about the effect of increasing the concentration of ethyl ethanoate on the position of equilibrium.

....

....

....

b Explain this effect using:

  i Le Chatelier's principle.

   ....

   ....

   ....

  ii The requirement that K_c is constant at constant temperature.

   ....

   ....

   ....

   ....

   ....

The titre for Tube 1 tells you the volume of alkali needed to neutralise the hydrochloric acid catalyst in each reaction mixture.

The equation for the reaction between ethanoic acid and sodium hydroxide is shown below:

$$CH_3COOH(aq) + NaOH(aq) \longrightarrow CH_3COO^-Na^+(aq) + H_2O(l)$$

For Tubes 2–6, the hydrochloric acid is a catalyst and therefore it does not change in mass or chemically. The extra alkali required is due to the formation of ethanoic acid.

Complete the following calculations on the results for the titration in Tube 2

c Calculate the volume of alkali required by control Tube 2 = ... cm³.

d Determine the [CH_3COOH].

  i Extra volume of alkali .... cm³

HINT

Subtract this value from all the other titre values to give the volume of alkali due to the ethanoic acid formed

59

ii Number of moles of CH_3COOH at equilibrium = No. of moles of ethanoic acid

= number of extra moles of alkali required = ... mol

iii Equilibrium concentration of CH_3COOH ($[CH_3COOH]_{eqm}$)

$= \dfrac{n}{V} =$ .... mol dm^{-3}

e Determine the $[C_2H_5OH]_{eqm}$.

$[C_2H_5OH]_{eqm} = \dfrac{n}{V} =$ .... mol dm^{-3}

f Calculate the equilibrium concentration of ethyl ethanoate.

i Calculate the initial number of moles of $CH_3COOC_2H_5$

Mass of $CH_3COOC_2H_5$ initially   = density × volume

= 0.900 × ....

= .... g

ii Calculate the number of moles of $CH_3COOC_2H_5$ that have reacted

Initial number of moles = $\dfrac{mass}{Mr}$

= .... mol

iii Calculate the number of moles of CH_3COOH formed.

∴ Number of moles of $CH_3COOC_2H_5$ that have reacted

= .... mol

iv Calculate the number of moles of $CH_3COOC_2H_5$ at equilibrium.

= initial number – number that reacted

= .... mol

v Calculate the equilibrium concentration of $CH_3COOC_2H_5$.

$= \dfrac{n}{V} =$ .... mol dm^{-3}

g Calculate the equilibrium concentration of water

i Initial mass of water = density x volume

Volume of water = ... cm^3

Mass of water = ... × .... g

ii Initial number of moles of water = $\dfrac{m}{Mr} =$ .... mol

iii Number of moles of water that react = number of moles of $CH_3COOC_2H_5$ that react

= .... mol

iv Number of moles of water at equilibrium = initial number – number that reacted

= .... mol

v ∴ Equilibrium concentration of water = $\dfrac{n}{V} =$ .... mol dm^{-3}

h Write the expression for K_c.

....

....

i Calculate the value of K_c in this experiment and give the units.

....

....

HINT

From the equation for each CH_3COOH formed there is one C_2H_5OH. Therefore, no. of moles of C_2H_5OH = no. of moles of CH_3COOH

60

HINT

Note [ester] = [ethyl ethanoate]

j Use the results from the titration in Tube 3 to complete the following calculations.

Calculate:

i The extra volume of NaOH required/cm³

....

....

ii The no. of moles of ethanoic acid at equilibrium/mol

....

....

iii $[CH_3COOH]_{eqm}$/mol dm⁻³

....

....

iv $[C_2H_5OH]_{eqm}$/mol dm⁻³

....

....

v Initial no. of moles of ester/mol

....

....

vi No. of moles of ester at equilibrium/mol

....

....

vii $[ester]_{eqm}$/mol dm⁻³

....

....

viii Initial no. of moles of water/mol

....

....

ix No. of moles of water at equilibrium/mol

....

....

x $[water]_{eqm}$/mol dm⁻³

....

....

xi K_c

....

....

k Use the results from the titration in Tube 4 to complete the following calculations.

Calculate:

i The extra volume of NaOH required/cm³

....

....

ii The no. of moles of ethanoic acid at equilibrium/mol

....

....

iii $[CH_3COOH]_{eqm}$ / mol dm⁻³

....

....

iv $[C_2H_5OH]_{eqm}$/ mol dm⁻³

....

....

v Initial no. of moles of ester/mol

....

....

vi No. of moles of ester at equilibrium/mol

....

....

vii $[ester]_{eqm}$/ mol dm⁻³

....

....

viii Initial no. of moles of water/mol

....

....

ix No. of moles of water at equilibrium/mol

....

....

x   [water]$_{eqm}$/mol dm^{-3}

....

....

xi K_c

....

....

l   Use the results from the titration in Tube 5 to complete the following calculations.

Calculate:

i   The extra volume of NaOH required/cm^3

....

....

ii   The no. of moles of ethanoic acid at equilibrium/mol

....

....

iii [CH$_3$COOH]$_{eqm}$ / mol dm^{-3}

....

....

iv   [C$_2$H$_5$OH]$_{eqm}$/ mol dm^{-3}

....

....

v   Initial no. of moles of ester/mol

....

....

vi   No. of moles of ester at equilibrium/mol

....

....

vii [ester]$_{eqm}$/ mol dm^{-3}

....

....

viii Initial no. of moles of water/mol

....

....

ix No. of moles of water at equilibrium/mol

....

....

x [water]$_{eqm}$/mol dm^{-3}

....

....

xi K_c

....

....

m Use the results from the titration in Tube 6 to complete the following calculations.

Calculate:

i The extra volume of NaOH required/cm^3

....

....

ii The no. of moles of ethanoic acid at equilibrium/mol

....

....

iii [CH$_3$COOH]$_{eqm}$ / mol dm^{-3}

....

....

iv [C$_2$H$_5$OH]$_{eqm}$/ mol dm^{-3}

....

....

v Initial no. of moles of ester/mol

....

....

vi No. of moles of ester at equilibrium/mol

....

....

vii [ester]$_{eqm}$/ mol dm^{-3}

....

....

viii Initial no. of moles of water/mol

....

....

ix No. of moles of water at equilibrium/mol

....

....

x $[water]_{eqm}$/mol dm^{-3}

....

....

xi K_c

....

....

Evaluation

n The accepted value for K_c is 0.22. Identify which of your determinations (if any) is incorrect.

....

....

o Calculate the average value for K_c from your results.

....

....

p Calculate the percentage error for your results.

....

....

Chapter 6:
Rates of reaction

Chapter outline

This chapter refers to Chapter 9: Rates of reaction in the coursebook

In this chapter you will complete investigations on:

- 6.1 Effects of concentration on rate of chemical reaction
- 6.2 Effects of temperature and a homogeneous catalyst on the rate of chemical reaction
- 6.3 Observed catalysed reaction

Practical investigation 6.1:
Effects of concentration on rate of chemical reaction

Introduction

The reaction between dilute hydrochloric acid and calcium carbonate produces carbon dioxide as shown by the following equation:

$$CaCO_3(s) + 2HCl(aq) \rightarrow CaCl_2(aq) + H_2O(l) + CO_2(g)$$

The rate of the reaction can be determined by following the rate at which carbon dioxide is produced.

Equipment

You will need:

- one of the two sets of apparatus for measuring gaseous volumes (see Skills chapter)
- three conical flasks with a capacity of 150 cm³ or three boiling tubes with a capacity of 40 cm³ • weighing boat • 10 cm³ graduated pipette for accurate measurement of hydrochloric acid volume • wash bottle of distilled water • dropper • stopwatch

Access to:

- hydrochloric acid in three different concentrations: $0.500 \, mol \, dm^{-3}$, $0.750 \, mol \, dm^{-3}$ and $1.00 \, mol \, dm^{-3}$. You will repeat the method three times. • small marble chips (2–4 mm)
- a top-pan balance reading to at least two decimal places

Safety considerations

- Make sure you have read the advice in the Safety section at the beginning of this book and listen to any advice from your teacher before carrying out this investigation.

- Wear eye protection at all times.

- The hydrochloric acid is an irritant at the concentrations in the experiment.

Method

1   Weigh out three samples of 1.00 g of calcium carbonate in the form of marble chips.

2   Set up the apparatus for gas collection as shown in the Skills chapter.

3   When the flask bung is inserted into the flask it takes up a certain volume. If the starting volume is not 0.00 cm³, there are two ways to deal with this:

   •   Measure the volume at the start and when you plot the graph subtract the starting value from the subsequent readings.

   •   Press the bung in and then detach the tube from the gas syringe. Push the piston in to the zero mark and then replace the tube.

4   For the first experiment, measure 16.0 cm³ of 0.500 mol dm⁻³ hydrochloric acid and add to the reaction vessel.

5   Add one of the samples of marble chips to the acid then replace the bung immediately and start the clock.

6   Take readings of the gas volume every 15 s for up to 6 minutes and then every 30 s after that until the reaction is complete.

7   Record your results in Table 6.1.

8   Repeat Steps 4–6 using 10.70 cm³ of 0.750 mol dm⁻³ hydrochloric acid and record your results in Table 6.2.

9   Repeat Steps 4–6 using 8.00 cm³ of 1.00 mol dm⁻³ hydrochloric acid and record your results in Table 6.3

> **HINT**
> When you select the chips try and make them of a similar size so that the surface area for each experiment is as identical as possible.

Results

Experiment 1

Time/s	0	15	30	45	60	75	90	105	120	135
Vol. of gas/cm³										
Time/s	150	165	180	195	210	225	240	255	270	285
Vol. of gas/cm³										
Time/s	300	330	360	390	420	450	480	510	540	570
Vol. of gas/cm³										

Table 6.1

Experiment 2

Time/s	0	15	30	45	60	75	90	105	120	135
Vol. of gas/cm³										
Time/s	150	165	180	195	210	225	240	255	270	285
Vol. of gas/cm³										
Time/s	300	330	360	390	420	450	480	510	540	570
Vol. of gas/cm³										

Table 6.2

Experiment 3

Time/s	0	15	30	45	60	75	90	105	120	135
Volume of gas/cm³										
Time/s	150	165	180	195	210	225	240	255	270	285
Volume of gas/cm³										
Time/s	300	330	360	390	420	450	480	510	540	570
Volume of gas/cm³										

Table 6.3

Data analysis

a Plot the results from Experiments 1–3. Each line should be plotted using a different colour or use different symbols to distinguish them.

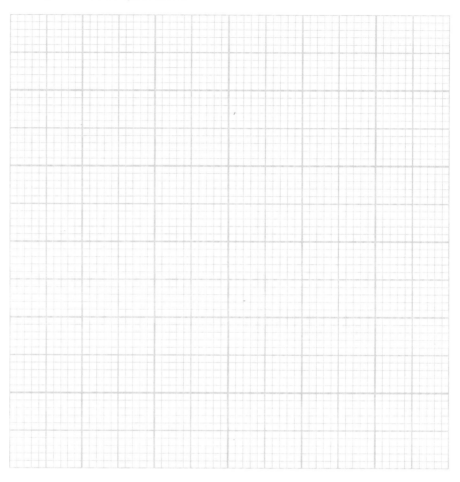

Evaluation

b Use your graphs to explain the following:

    i The effect of increasing the concentration of hydrochloric acid on the reaction rate.

    ....

    ....

    ....

    ....

    ii The final volume of gas produced.

    ....

    ....

    ....

c   Draw tangents at t = 0 for each line. What do their slopes show?

....

....

HINT

Assume 1 mol
of gas occupies
24 000 cm³

d   Calculate the following quantities for Experiments 1–3:

   i   The initial rate of reaction in terms of cm³ of carbon dioxide gas formed per minute.

   ii   The initial rate of reaction in terms of cm³ of carbon dioxide gas formed per second.

   iii The initial rate of reaction in terms of moles of carbon dioxide gas formed per second.

   iv   The initial rate of reaction in terms of change in number of moles of hydrochloric acid per second.

Record your answers in Table 6.4.

$[HCl(aq)]/$ $mol\,dm^{-3}$	Rate – production of CO_2 $cm^3\,min^{-1}$	Rate – production of $CO_2/cm^3\,s^{-1}$	Rate – production of $CO_2/mol\,s^{-1}$	Rate – removal of $HCl(aq)/mol\,s^{-1}$
0.500				
0.750				
1.00				

Table 6.4

e   Plot a graph of concentration of HCl(aq) (horizontal axis) against rate of reaction in terms of change in decrease of moles of HCl acid per second.

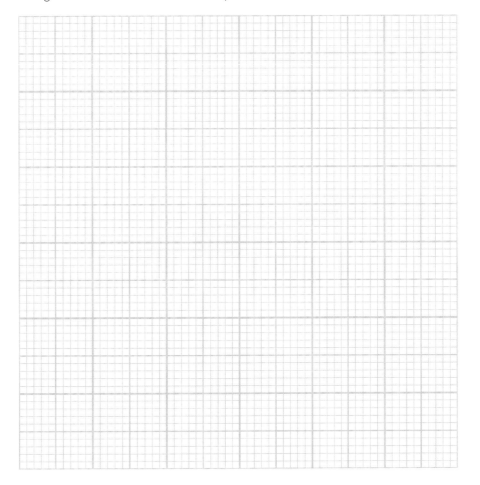

f **About** which of your points can you be absolutely confident. Explain your answer.

……

……

g Explain what the graph shows.

……

……

h What could you do to be more confident about your conclusion? Explain your answer.

……

……

……

i In the space provided create a table and record:

- The control variables that were kept constant
- For each variable explain how it was kept constant.

Practical investigation 6.2:
Effects of temperature and a homogeneous catalyst on the rate of chemical reaction

Introduction

In this investigation you will observe the reaction between manganate(VII) ions and ethanedioate ions. Your observations will help you to make deductions about the reaction. You will also plan and then carry out a final part of this investigation.

The reaction between acidified manganate (VII) ions and ethanedioate ions is described by the reaction:

$$2MnO_4^-(aq) + 5C_2O_4^{2-}(aq) + 16H^+(aq) \rightarrow 2Mn^{2+}(aq) + 10CO_2(aq) + 8H_2O(l)$$

manganate(VII)   ethanedioate

Equipment

You will need:

- six test tubes   • test-tube rack   • Bunsen burner and heat-resistant pad   • four droppers
- permanent marker pen   • anti-bumping granules

Access to:

- $0.0200 \, mol \, dm^{-3}$ potassium manganate(VII) solution   • $0.100 \, mol \, dm^{-3}$ potassium or sodium ethanedioate solution   • $1 \, mol \, dm^{-3}$ sulfuric acid   • $0.100 \, mol \, dm^{-3}$ manganese(II) sulfate solution

Safety considerations

- Make sure you have read the advice in the Safety section at the beginning of this book and listen to any advice from your teacher before carrying out this investigation.

- Wear eye protection throughout the experiment.

- The sulfuric acid is an irritant at this concentration.

- The manganate(VII) solution leaves brown stains on clothing and skin. Handle with care!

Method

1   Collect samples of the four solutions provided and place in labelled test tubes for use during your experiment.

2   In a clean test tube, add sodium ethanedioate (sodium oxalate) solution to a depth of 2 cm, then add an equal volume of $1 \, mol \, dm^{-3}$ sulfuric acid.

3   Add some anti-bumping granules to the mixture.

4   Add 2–3 drops of potassium manganate(VII) solution. Describe and record your observations.

....

....

....

5   Heat the mixture. Describe and record what happens.

....

....

Data analysis

a   Explain your observations at Steps 4 and 5.

   i   Step 4

....

....

ii Step 5

....

....

Evaluation

b Describe a method you could use to more accurately show what happens in the reaction. Explain why you would use this method.

....

....

c Describe how you could investigate whether this statement is correct.

The manganese(II) ion ($Mn^{2+}(aq)$) is thought to catalyse the reaction.

....

....

d Carry out your method and describe your observations.

....

....

....

e Explain your observations.

....

....

....

Practical investigation 6.3:
Observed catalysed reaction

Introduction

Your teacher will demonstrate this reaction. Platinum wire is the catalyst.

This reaction is the first step in the manufacture of nitric acid from ammonia.

$$4NH_3(g) + 5O_2(g) \rightarrow 4NO(g) + 6H_2O(g)$$

Evaluation

a   During the experimental demonstration write down your observations. Then use them to answer the questions which follow.

....

....

....

....

b   Provide two pieces of evidence that show a reaction is taking place in the flask.

....

....

c   What type of catalysis is taking place? Explain your answer.

....

....

d   What evidence is there that the reaction occurs on the surface of the catalyst?

....

....

Chapter 7:
The properties of metals

Chapter outline

This chapter relates to Chapter 10: Periodicity and Chapter 11: Group 2 in the coursebook.

In this chapter you will complete investigations on:

- 7.1 Properties of metal oxides and metal chlorides across Period 3
- 7.2 Relative atomic mass of magnesium using a back-titration method
- 7.3 Separation of two metal ions in solution
- 7.4 Identification of three metal compounds using qualitative analysis

Practical investigation 7.1:
Properties of metal oxides and metal chlorides across Period 3

Introduction

In this practical, you will investigate the reactions of metal oxides and metal chlorides with water. From the results, you can establish trends and deduce properties as you move across Period 3 from left to right.

Equipment

You will need:

- test tubes and a test tube rack   • a dropper   • Universal Indicator (U.I.) paper   • small spatula (e.g. Nuffield type)   • wash bottle filled with distilled water   • a dropper bottle of Universal Indicator

Access to:

- a solution of sodium hydroxide solution   • solid magnesium oxide   • solid aluminium oxide
- anhydrous magnesium chloride   • anhydrous aluminium chloride   • sodium chloride

---

Safety considerations

- Make sure you have read the advice in the Safety section at the beginning of this book and listen to any advice from your teacher before carrying out this investigation.

- Eye protection must be worn at all times during the investigation.

- In some reactions a certain amount of heat may be generated. This should be taken into consideration.

- Any gases evolved should not be inhaled and residual solids and liquids should be emptied down the sink using plenty of water.

- The Universal Indicator is dissolved in ethanol and is therefore flammable.

Part 1: Testing metal oxides

Method

1 Take three test tubes and carry out the following additions using the instructions in Table 7.1.

Test tube	1st addition	2nd addition	3rd addition
I Na_2O	Distilled water to a depth of 3 cm	Five drops of sodium hydroxide solution	3–4 drops of Universal Indicator solution
II MgO	Distilled water to a depth of 3 cm	A small spatula measure of magnesium oxide solid	
III Al_2O_3	Distilled water to a depth of 3 cm	A small spatula measure of aluminium oxide	

Table 7.1

2 Record your observations in Table 7.2.

Results

Test tube	Observations	Conclusions
I Na_2O		
II MgO		
III Al_2O_3		

Table 7.2

Data analysis

a What is the acid–base nature of the metal oxides as you go across Period 3 from left to right?

....

....

....

b Write equations for the reactions (if any) between each of the metal oxides and water.

  i Sodium hydroxide

  ....

  ii Magnesium oxide

  ....

  iii Aluminium oxide

  ....

Part 2: Testing metal chlorides

Method

1 Take three test tubes and carry out the following additions using the instructions in Table 7.3.

Test tube	1st addition	2nd addition	3rd addition
NaCl	Distilled water to a depth of 3 cm	A small spatula measure of solid sodium chloride solid	3–4 drops of Universal Indicator solution. If any gas is evolved then test with moist Universal Indicator paper.
$MgCl_2$	Distilled water to a depth of 3 cm	A small spatula measure of solid magnesium chloride	
$AlCl_3$	Distilled water to a depth of 3 cm	A small spatula measure of solid aluminium chloride	

Table 7.3

2 Record your observations in Table 7.4.

Results

Test tube	Observations	Conclusions
NaCl		
$MgCl_2$		
$AlCl_3$		

Table 7.4

Data analysis

c What is the trend in the nature of the chemical bonding of the metal chlorides as you go across Period 3 from left to right? Explain your answer.

....

....

....

....

....

d Write equations for the reactions (if any) for each of the three metal chlorides with water. If you are not sure of your answer then try researching the internet.

i Sodium chloride

....

ii Magnesium chloride

....

iii Aluminium chloride

....

Practical Investigation 7.2:
Relative atomic mass of magnesium using a back-titration method

Introduction

In this practical you will use a method called back titration. This consists of adding a known, excess amount of acid to a measured mass of magnesium ribbon and then finding how much of the acid has reacted by titrating the excess acid against standard sodium hydroxide.

The equation for the reaction is: $Mg(s) + 2HCl(aq) \rightarrow MgCl_2(aq) + H_2(g)$

Equipment

You will need:

• 50 cm³ burette • a small glass funnel for filling burette • a larger glass funnel for preventing loss of acid spray • a white tile for titration • 25 cm³ pipette • pipette filler • a pair of scissors • a ruler • 50 cm³ pipette or 25 cm³ measuring cylinder • 250 cm³ conical flask for the reaction vessel and for the titrations • dropper bottle filled with methyl orange indicator

Access to:

• standard 0.500 mol dm⁻³ hydrochloric acid • standard 0.100 mol dm⁻³ sodium hydroxide solution • magnesium ribbon • steel wool • top-pan balance reading to three decimal places

---

Safety considerations

- Make sure you have read the advice in the Safety section at the beginning of this book and listen to any advice from your teacher before carrying out this investigation.

- Eye protection must be worn at all times.

- The sodium hydroxide is an irritant at the concentration provided.

- When the magnesium reacts with the acid there is some acid spray formed but this is minimised by using the glass filter funnel.

- When filling the burette with the standard alkali solution, care must be taken. Refer to Skills chapter if you are unsure.

- Methyl orange is poisonous. It should be washed off skin immediately.

Method

1 Measure out 50 cm^3 of 0.500 mol dm^{-3} hydrochloric acid into the 250 cm^3 conical flask. This can be done using the 50 cm^3 pipette or the 25 cm^3 measuring cylinder.

2 Measure out a 12 cm length of magnesium ribbon and carefully clean it with a small piece of steel wool.

3 From this 12 cm length, accurately cut a 10 cm length and weigh it. Record the mass in the results section.

4 Cut this 10 cm length into smaller lengths and place them all in the 250 cm^3 conical flask.

5 Using either 50 cm^3 pipette or the measuring cylinder measure out 50 cm^3 of the 0.500 mol dm^{-3} hydrochloric acid.

6 Add it to the magnesium ribbon in the flask.

7 Immediately place the larger glass funnel in the mouth of the flask to minimise the escape of any acid spray.

8 Swirl the flask carefully making sure that all the magnesium ribbon dissolves in the acid.

9 Carefully rinse any acid spray on the glass funnel back into the flask using distilled water from your wash bottle.

10 Transfer the contents to a 250 cm^3 volumetric flask and make up to 250 cm^3 with distilled water. See the Skills chapter for full instructions on how to do this.

11 Fill the burette with the standard 0.100 mol dm^{-3} sodium hydroxide solution.

12 Titrate 25 cm^3 samples of the reaction mixture against the sodium hydroxide solution.

13 Add 2–3 drops of the methyl orange indicator.

14 Record your results in Table 7.5.

Results

Mass of magnesium ribbon = …………………………g

Burette reading/cm³	Rough	1	2	3
2nd				
1st				
Titre/cm³				

Table 7.5

Data analysis

a Record the volume of sodium hydroxide required to neutralise 25.00 cm³ of the diluted reaction mixture: …………………… cm³

b Calculate the number of moles of hydrochloric acid present in 25.00 cm³ sample of reaction mixture.

………

………

c Calculate the total number of moles of acid **remaining after the reaction** with the magnesium.

………

………

d Calculate the number of moles of hydrochloric acid at the start and from this calculate the **number of moles of hydrochloric acid that reacted**.

………

………

………

………

e Write the equation for the reaction of hydrochloric acid with the magnesium ribbon.

………

f Calculate the number of moles of magnesium present in the reaction.

………

………

………

………

HINT

$$A_r = \frac{mass}{n}$$

g Calculate the relative atomic mass of magnesium.

....

....

....

....

Evaluation

h Identify any steps in the procedure where you think errors can occur.

....

....

....

....

Practical investigation 7.3: Planning
Separation of two metal ions in solution

Introduction

You will plan and then carry out an investigation to separate the magnesium ions from a mixture of magnesium and barium ions in solution. You will then identify the magnesium ions.

> ### Equipment
>
> **You will need:**
>
> • two boiling tubes and one test tube • test-tube rack • filter funnel and filter paper
> • two droppers • a wash bottle filled with distilled water
>
> **Access to:**
>
> • a solution containing barium and magnesium ions • 1.00 mol dm^{-3} sodium hydroxide solution • 0.500 mol dm^{-3} sodium sulfate solution

Safety considerations

• Make sure you have read the advice in the Safety section at the beginning of this book and listen to any advice from your teacher before carrying out this investigation.

• The mixture contains barium ions, which are toxic. Any spillages must be wiped down with plenty of water and washed from the skin immediately.

• The sodium hydroxide solution is an irritant at the concentration provided.

Method

Table 7.6 shows the solubility of the hydroxides and sulfates of magnesium and barium.

Metal	Solubility of hydroxide/mol dm^{-3}	Solubility of sulfate/mol dm^{-3}
Magnesium	2×10^{-4}	1.83
Barium	1.5×10^{-1}	9.43×10^{-6}

Table 7.6

Using the information in Table 7.6, describe a method to separate the barium ions from the magnesium ions leaving the magnesium ions in solution.

1 Step 1:

....

....

2 Explanation:

....

....

3 Step 2:

....

....

4 Explanation:

....

....

5 Describe a method to confirm the identity of the magnesium ions.

....

....

....

6 Complete your investigation. Record your observations in Table 7.7.

Results

Step	Observations
1	....
2	....
Identification	....

Table 7.7

Data analysis

a For each of the steps in Table 7.7, give the **ionic** equation for the reactions taking place.

....

....

Evaluation

b Was your method successful? Explain your answer.

....

....

....

....

c Outline a method you could use to separate the two ions and finish with $Ba^{2+}(aq)$ ions in solution.

....

....

....

....

Practical investigation 7.4:
Identification of three metal compounds using qualitative analysis

Introduction

In this investigation, you are asked to identify three compounds of the same Group 2 metal using chemical tests. Each compound contains three elements.

Equipment

You will need:

• five test tubes, two boiling tubes and a test-tube rack • four droppers • filter funnel and three filter papers • Bunsen burner and heat-resistant pad • wooden splint • wash bottle filled with distilled water

Access to:

• samples of compounds A, B and C to test • 2.00 mol dm^{-3} hydrochloric acid • 1.00 mol dm^{-3} nitric acid • lime water • Universal Indicator (U.I.) solution • a fume cupboard

Safety considerations

- Make sure you have read the advice in the Safety section at the beginning of this book and listen to any advice from your teacher before carrying out this investigation.

- Eye protection must be worn at all times during the investigation.

- During the heating of any solids do not inhale any gases evolved and place the test tube in the fume cupboard.

- The Universal Indicator is dissolved in ethanol and is therefore flammable.

- The lime water is an irritant.

- The acids are irritants at the concentrations provided.

Part 1: Investigating compound A

Method

1 Add one spatula measure of compound A to a test tube. Add a few drops of dilute hydrochloric acid and test any gases evolved. Record your observations and conclusions.

   ....

2 Add one spatula measure of compound A to a boiling tube and to it add 5 cm³ of dilute nitric acid to a depth of 5 cm. Record your observations and conclusions.

   ....

3 Heat the mixture gently and then filter into another boiling tube. Keep the filtrate. Record your observations and conclusions.

   ....

4 Add dilute sodium hydroxide solution to the filtrate formed. Record your observations and conclusions.

   ....

Data analysis

a Provide equations for the reactions taking place at each of the steps 1–4

   ....

   ....

   ....

b Identify compound A

   ....

Part 2: Investigating compound B

Method

1   Add a small spatula measure of compound B to a clean test tube.

2   Add distilled water to B, mix thoroughly. Record your observations and conclusions.

    ....

3   Add a few drops of Universal Indicator solution to the mixture. Record your observations and conclusions.

    ....

Data analysis

c   Provide equations for reactions taking place

    ....

    ....

d   Identify compound B

    ....

Part 3: Investigating compound C

Method

1   Add a small spatula measure of compound C to a test tube and add distilled water. Mix thoroughly. Record your observations and conclusions.

    ....

2   Add a few drops of Universal Indicator solution to the mixture. Record your observations and conclusions.

    ....

3   Add a small spatula measure of compound C to a clean, dry test tube.

4   Heat the compound and test any gases evolved. Record your observations and conclusions.

    ....

Data analysis

e Provide equations for reactions taking place

....

....

f Identify compound C

....

....

Chapter 8:
The properties of non-metals

Chapter outline

This chapter relates to Chapter 12: Group 17, and Chapter 13: Nitrogen and sulfur in the coursebook.

In this chapter you will complete investigations on:

- 8.1 Formula of hydrated sodium thiosulfate crystals
- 8.2 Preparation and properties of the hydrogen halides
- 8.3 Reaction of bromine with sulfite ions (sulfate (IV))
- 8.4 Identification of unknowns containing halide ions

Practical investigation 8.1:
Formula of hydrated sodium thiosulfate crystals

Introduction

You will carry out a titration in order to find the value of x in the formula $Na_2S_2O_3.xH_2O$ for hydrated sodium thiosulfate. The concentration of the thiosulfate ion ($S_2O_3^{2-}$) can be determined by titrating it against iodine liberated from the reaction between standard copper(II) sulfate and iodide ions. The two relevant reactions are:

Reaction 1: $\qquad 2Cu^{2+}(aq) + 4I^-(aq) \rightarrow 2CuI(s) + I_2(aq)$

Reaction 2: $\qquad 2S_2O_3^{2-}(aq) + I_2(aq) \rightarrow S_4O_6^{2-}(aq) + 2I^-(aq)$

Equipment

You will need:

- 150 cm³ conical flask • 2 x 250 cm³ volumetric flasks • 1% starch indicator and dropper
- wash bottle filled with distilled water • burette stand • 25.0 cm³ pipette • pipette filler
- white tile • 250 cm³ beaker and 100 cm³ beaker • stirring rod • small dropper • small filter funnel for burette and larger one for volumetric flask • 10 cm³ measuring cylinder

Access to:

- copper(II) sulfate solution • 0.100 mol dm⁻³ hydrochloric acid • sodium thiosulfate solution
- 0.500 mol dm⁻³ potassium iodide solution • a two or three place top-pan balance

---

Safety considerations

- Make sure you have read the advice in the Safety section at the beginning of this book and listen to any advice from your teacher before carrying out this investigation.

- The copper(II) sulfate solution is harmful and is an environmental hazard.

Method

Part 1: Preparation of solutions

Refer to Skills chapter to remind you of how to make up a standard solution.

1 **a** Weigh out between 3.11 g and 3.13 g of $CuSO_4.5H_2O$.

Mass of $CuSO_4.5H_2O$ = ... g

b Dissolve the solid in distilled water and make up to 250 cm³ in a volumetric flask.

2 **a** Weigh out between 6.20 g and 6.22 g of sodium thiosulfate crystals.

Mass of sodium thiosulfate crystals .... g

b Dissolve the solid in distilled water and make up to 250 cm³ in a volumetric flask.

Part 2: Titration

Refer to Skills chapter to remind you of how to do a titration

1 Fill the burette to the zero mark using your sodium thiosulfate solution.

2 Using a pipette add 25.00 cm³ of your copper(II) sulfate solution to a 150 cm³ conical flask.

3 Add 10 cm³ of the potassium iodide solution. You will see a reaction take place. This is **Reaction 1**. The white precipitate formed is copper (I) iodide.

4 Carry out the titration using starch indicator to show the end-point of the reaction. This is **Reaction 2**.

IMPORTANT – the starch indicator should **not** be added immediately. The colour of the iodine will gradually fade. You add it when the colour is pale-straw or pale-yellow. When you add the starch, the mixture will go blue/black in colour. The end-point is when the blue/black colour disappears.

5 Do one rough titration followed by complete accurate titrations until you have two titres which are within 0.100 cm³ of each other. Record your results in Table 8.1. (You need to add relevant column headings.)

Results

Table 8.1

Data analysis

a Identify the concordant titres and give the average of these values.

Conncordant titres = ...cm³ and ....cm³

Average of concordant titres = ...cm³

b Using the equation for Reaction 1 (see Introduction) calculate how many moles of copper(II) ion are needed to form 1 mol of iodine.

....

c Using the equation for Reaction 2 calculate how many moles of sodium thiosulfate react with 1 mol of iodine.

....

d Using these two results, calculate the number of moles of thiosulfate ion that are equivalent to 1 mol of copper(II) ion.

....

Evaluation

e Calculate

i The number of moles of copper(II) ion present in 25.00 cm³ of solution.

....

....

ii The number of moles of thiosulfate ion present in the reaction and then the number of moles of thiosulfate ion present in 250 cm³ of solution.

....

....

....

....

iii Use these results to calculate the relative formula mass of sodium thiosulfate and the value of x in the formula $Na_2S_2O_3.xH_2O$.

....

....

....

....

....

Practical investigation 8.2:
Preparation and properties of the hydrogen halides

Introduction

In this investigation, you will prepare hydrogen chloride, hydrogen bromide and hydrogen iodide. You will then investigate the chemical reactions.

Equipment

You will need:

- approximately 15 **dry** test tubes and a test-tube rack • stoppers or corks for test tubes • three **dry** boiling tubes • three right-angled glass delivery tubes (see Figure 8.1) • plastic gloves • Bunsen burner, heat-resistant pad and straight tongs • small spatula • short length of nichrome wire • thin glass stirring rod • paper towels • retort stand, boss and clamp • 250 cm^3 beaker

Access to:

- concentrated phosphoric acid • nitric acid • silver nitrate solution • phosphorus(V) oxide / phosphorus pentoxide solid • Universal Indicator (U.I.) solution in a dropper bottle • solid potassium chloride • solid potassium bromide • solid potassium iodide • concentrated ammonia solution in a small dropper bottle • a top-pan balance

---

Safety considerations

- Make sure you have read the advice in the Safety section at the beginning of this book and listen to any advice from your teacher before carrying out this investigation.

- Safety goggles must be worn at all times.

- Both the concentrated phosphoric acid and phosphorus(V) oxide are corrosive and should be treated with great care.

- The ammonia is a highly pungent gas and it is best to test its reaction with the hydrogen halides in a fume cupboard.

- The hydrogen halide fumes themselves are harmful and should not be inhaled.

- At the end of the experiment, the boiling tubes should be placed in the fume cupboard where they can be washed up.

Method

Part 1: Preparation and collection of gas of each hydrogen halide

1   The apparatus set-up is shown in Figure 8.1. For each hydrogen halide, place approximately 2.00 g of the solid metal halide in a boiling tube along with approximately 1.00 g of phosphorus(V) oxide solid.

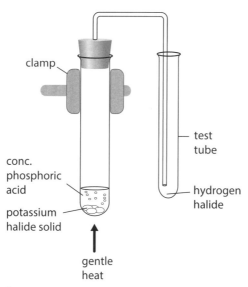

Figure 8.1

2   Then add approximately 2.00 cm³ of concentrated phosphoric acid.

3   As soon as the acid has been added, place the bung in the neck of the boiling tube **gently** and heat the mixture.

4   The collecting test tube is filled with hydrogen halide gas when misty fumes can be seen escaping from the neck of the collecting tube or if you blow gently across the neck of the tube and you can see misty fumes.

5   As soon as each tube is full of gas it should be stoppered. You will need to collect at least four test tubes of gas of each hydrogen halide to complete Part 2 of this investigation.

Part 2: Testing the chemical reactions of the three hydrogen halides

1   **a**   Fill a 250 cm³ beaker $\frac{2}{3}$ with water.

    b   For each hydrogen halide, take Test tube 1 filled with gas, turn upside down and remove the stopper under the water. Record your observations in Table 8.2.

    c   Add a few drops of Universal Indicator to the solution formed. Record all observations in Table 8.2.

2   **a**   Take Test tube 2 of gas over to the fume cupboard.

    b   Dip the stirring rod into the solution of concentrated ammonia.

    c   Remove the stopper of the test tube and lower the wet end of the stirring rod into the test tube. Record your observations in Table 8.2.

3   **a**   Using the tongs, hold the nichrome wire in a hot Bunsen flame until it glows red hot.

    b   Remove the stopper from Test tube 3 and lower the hot nichrome wire into the tube. Record your observations in Table 8.2

4   **a**   Remove the stopper from Test tube 4 and very quickly add a few drops of nitric acid followed by silver nitrate solution. Replace the stopper and shake the tube vigorously with the mixture of liquids. Record your observations in Table 8.2.

    b   To the resulting mixture, add a few drops of dilute ammonia solution.

    c   Then add a few drops of concentrated ammonia solution.

    d   Record your observations at each stage in Table 8.2.

5 Repeat Steps 1–4 for each of your three hydrogen halides you have collected.

Results

Hydrogen halide gas	Observations			
	Test tube 1: upside down test tube in water	Test tube 2: reaction with ammonia	Test tube 3: action of heat	Test tube 4: silver nitrate
HCl	....			
HBr	....			
HI	....			

Table 8.2

Data analysis

a Write the equation for the preparation of a hydrogen halide. Use HX to stand for all three hydrogen halides.

....

Evaluation

b Explain your observations for the upside down test tubes in water. Write a general equation for the reaction.

....

....

....

c Explain the reactions (if any) with ammonia. Write a general equation for the reaction.

....

....

d Explain the changes (if any) when the heat was applied to each hydrogen halide. Give an equation for any reaction.

....

....

e Explain the separate observations with silver nitrate and give a general ionic equation for the three reactions taking place.

....

....

....

....

....

Practical investigation 8.3:
Reaction of bromine with sulfite ions (sulfate (IV))

Introduction

You will investigate the reaction between aqueous bromine and sulfite ions (sulfate (IV)).

Equipment

You will need:

• boiling tube • three test tubes and a test-tube rack • two droppers • plastic gloves • small spatula • wash bottle filled with distilled water • 10 cm³ measuring cylinder

Access to:

• bromine water • solid sodium sulfite • barium chloride solution • $2.00 \, mol \, dm^{-3}$ hydrochloric acid • $2.00 \, mol \, dm^{-3}$ nitric acid • $0.100 \, mol \, dm^{-3}$ silver nitrate solution • $2.00 \, mol \, dm^{-3}$ ammonia solution • concentrated ammonia solution

---

Safety considerations

• Make sure you have read the advice in the Safety section at the beginning of this book and listen to any advice from your teacher before carrying out this investigation.

• The bromine water is harmful and should not be held near the nose or face at any time.

• All of the acids are irritants at the concentrations provided.

• The silver nitrate is an irritant at the concentration provided.

- Solutions of barium ions are toxic. The barium chloride should be handled with care and, if possible, plastic gloves should be worn.

Method

1 Add one spatula measure of solid sodium sulfite to the boiling tube and to it add $10\,cm^3$ of distilled water. Shake the mixture until the solid has dissolved.

2 Take approximately $5.00\,cm^3$ of the sodium sulfite solution and add it to a fresh test tube.

3 Add a few drops of bromine water and mix thoroughly. Record your observations in Table 8.3.

4 Divide the reaction mixture into two equal portions (I and II).

5 To reaction mixture portion I:

   a add 2–3 drops of barium chloride solution. Record your observations in Table 8.3 .

   b then add five drops of dilute hydrochloric acid and shake carefully. Record your observations.

6 To reaction mixture portion II:

   a add two drops of nitric acid, followed by two drops of silver nitrate solution.

   b then add three drops of dilute ammonia solution and three drops of concentrated ammonia solution. Record your observations in Table 8.3.

Results

Reaction	Observations
Step 3 Bromine water + sodium sulfite solution	....
Step 5: Portion I Addition of barium chloride solution followed by dilute hydrochloric acid	....
Step 6: Portion II Addition of silver nitrate and nitric acid followed by dilute ammonia solution, then conc. ammonia solution	....

Table 8.3

Data analysis

a Explain how you could tell that a reaction occurred at Step 3 of the method.

....

b What conclusions can you draw about one of the products of this reaction? Provide the ionic equation for the reaction that occurs at this step.

....

....

....

c What product is detected at Step 5? Explain your answer and provide an ionic equation for the reaction that occurs.

....

....

....

Evaluation

d Write the ionic equation for the reaction between bromine and sulfite ions. Show your working by giving the oxidation numbers of the reactants and products and the oxidation number changes.

....

....

....

e Using oxidation numbers explain why this is a redox reaction

....

....

....

Practical investigation 8.4:
Identification of unknowns containing halide ions

Introduction

You will carry out specific tests on three unknown compounds that contain halide ions and use the results to identify the ions present. All three compounds contain the same cation.

Equipment

You will need:

- five test tubes plus stoppers • test-tube rack • Bunsen burner and heat-resistant pad
- three graduated droppers • Universal Indicator (U.I.) paper • wash bottle filled with distilled water • small spatula

Access to:

- unknown solids labelled x, y and z • $2.00\,mol\,dm^{-3}$ sodium hydroxide solution • $2.00\,mol\,dm^{-3}$ ammonia solution (dilute ammonia solution) • concentrated ammonia solution • $0.100\,mol\,dm^{-3}$ silver nitrate solution • cyclohexane • chlorine water (saturated) • fume cupboard

---

Safety considerations

- Make sure you have read the advice in the Safety section at the beginning of this book and listen to any advice from your teacher before carrying out this investigation.

- The sodium hydroxide solution is corrosive at the concentration provided.

- The concentrated ammonia solution is harmful and should not be taken out of the fume cupboard.

- Cyclohexane vapour is harmful. Do not dispose of this down the sink. Use the reagent bottle available and decant the upper layer into this bottle.

- The silver nitrate is an irritant.

- The chlorine water is a saturated solution and will release chlorine gas, which is toxic. Avoid inhalation. As with the concentrated ammonia, it should be kept in the fume cupboard or in a stoppered boiling tube.

Method

1. Take a sample of unknown solid X and add to a dry test tube. Add about $1\,cm^3$ of sodium hydroxide solution and heat gently. Test any gases evolved using moist Universal Indicator paper. Record all your observations in Table 8.4.

2. To half a small spatula measure of X, add $3\,cm^3$ of distilled water. Make sure the solid is dissolved. Add five drops of chlorine water to the solution. If there is a reaction, add about $1\,cm^3$ of cyclohexane, stopper the test tube and carefully shake the mixture.

Now repeat Steps 1 and 2 for unknown compounds Y and Z.

3 **a** Add 2–3 crystals of X to a test tube, followed by 3 cm³ of distilled water.

   b Add 1–2 drops of silver nitrate solution.

   c Add the appropriate ammonia solution to confirm the identity of the halide ion.

Now repeat Step 3 for unknown compounds Y and Z.

Results

Method step	Observations of unknowns		
	X	Y	Z
1			
2			
3			
Amount and concentration ammonia solution added			

Table 8.4

Data analysis

a Name and give the formula of the cation in compounds X, Y and Z.

....

b Explain how you arrived at your answer and provide any appropriate equations.

....

....

c   Name and give the formula of the halide ion in X.

....

d   Give two pieces of evidence for your answer to (c) and for each piece of evidence give an ionic equation to support your answer.

....

....

....

....

....

e   Name and give the formula of the halide ion in Y.

....

f   Give two pieces of evidence for your answer and for each piece of evidence give an ionic equation to support your answer.

....

....

....

....

....

g   Name and give the formula of the halide ion in Z.

....

h   Give two pieces of evidence for your answer and for each piece of evidence give an ionic equation to support your answer.

....

....

....

....

....

Chapter outline

This chapter relates to Chapter 15: Hydrocarbons and Chapter 16: Halogenoalkanes in the coursebook.

In this chapter you will complete investigations on:

- 9.1 Cracking of hydrocarbons
- 9.2 How halogenoalkane structure affects the rate of hydrolysis

Practical investigation 9.1:
Cracking of hydrocarbons

Introduction

In this investigation you will carry out the thermal decomposition (cracking) of a long chain alkane (paraffin oil).

Equipment

You will need:

• Bunsen burner, tripod and gauze • heat-resistant mat. • heat-resistant test tube (e.g. Pyrex®) • Delivery tube plus stopper. The delivery tube has a Bunsen valve at the end (see Figure 9.1) • small trough • several (at least five) test tubes plus stoppers • wooden splint • dropper • spatula • retort stand, boss and clamp • plastic (vinyl) gloves for handling the ceramic wool

Access to:

• paraffin oil • ceramic wool • bromine water • broken pot

Safety considerations

- Make sure you have read the advice in the Safety section at the beginning of this book and listen to any advice from your teacher before carrying out this investigation.

- You will be heating a test tube to very high temperatures. You must allow several minutes for the apparatus to cool down.

- Bromine water is harmful and must be handled with care.

- There is danger of suck-back. The Bunsen valve is designed to minimise this danger but does not eliminate the risk of it happening. If suck-back starts, lift the retort stand so that the delivery tube is out of the water but **continue to heat** the test tube until the water is driven out of the tube.

- The products of cracking can cause irritation to airways. When smelling the products, the vapour must be gently 'wafted' towards the nose rather than inhaled.

- Ceramic wool can cause skin irritation and plastic gloves should be worn when handling it.

Part 1: Testing the paraffin oil before cracking

Method

1 In the space provided, draw a results table (Table 9.1) for recording your observations during this practical.

2 Carefully smell the paraffin oil and record your observations in Table 9.1.

3 Add some paraffin oil to a test tube and add a few drops of bromine water. Shake thoroughly and record your observations.

4 Place some ceramic wool on a piece of gauze on a tripod. Add a few drops of paraffin oil to the ceramic wool and hold a lit splint close to the ceramic wool. Record your observations in Table 9.1.

Results

Create your own results table for this investigation with appropriate column headings in the space provided.

Table 9.1

Data analysis

a Explain what your observations tell you about the usefulness of paraffin oil as:

 i A fuel

  ....

  ....

 ii As a starting material for polymerisation.

  ....

  ....

Part 2: Cracking the paraffin oil

Method

1 Using a dropper, add paraffin oil to a depth of 1–2 cm to a clean dry heat-resistant test tube. Try to make sure that the oil does not run down the sides of the test tube.

2 Take some ceramic wool and push it to the bottom of the test tube so that it absorbs the paraffin oil.

3 Using a spatula, add come pieces of broken pot to the test tube. Spread it out in the tube to maximise the surface area of the pot.

4 Set up the apparatus as shown in Figure 9.1. Place five test tubes in the trough so that they are full of water; have stoppers ready for the test tubes.

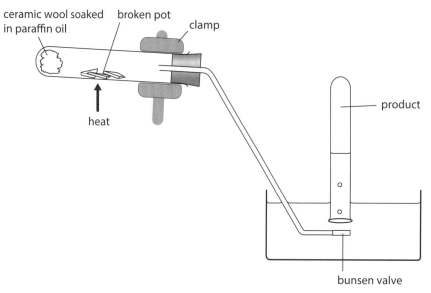

Figure 9.1

5 Heat the broken pot very strongly. The first bubbles of gas coming from the delivery tube will be air expelled from the heated test tube and for this reason the first test tube of gas should be discarded.

6 Once the broken pot is very hot, start collecting the gas coming from the tube. If the flow of gas becomes very slow, heat the ceramic wool for a second or two to vaporise more of the paraffin oil and then continue to heat the broken pot.

7 Once you have collected five test tubes of gaseous product, use the retort stand to lift the test tube and delivery tube away from the trough. Continue heating until no water is present in the delivery tube. The tube should be carefully carried over to the fume cupboard so that the products are not emitted into the laboratory.

Part 3: Testing the products of cracking

Method

1 Complete the following tests: record your observations in Table 9.1.

   a Smell: remove a stopper from one of the test tubes and waft the gas towards your nose.

   b Combustion: remove a stopper from one of the test tubes and place a lighted wooden splint near the mouth of the test tube.

   c Bromine water: remove a stopper from one of the test tubes and quickly add about 1 cm^3 of bromine water.

Data analysis

b Explain what your observations tell you about the usefulness of the product(s) as:

i A fuel

....

....

....

ii A starting material for polymerisation.

....

....

c Summarise your results and explain the economic importance of cracking.

....

....

....

....

Practical investigation 9.2:
How halogenoalkane structure affects the rate of hydrolysis

Introduction

This practical investigates how halogenoalkane structure (e.g. primary (1°), secondary (2°) or tertiary (3°)) affects the rate of hydrolysis.

Equipment

You will need:

• 250 cm³ beaker • -10 to 110°C thermometer • six test tubes and three stoppers • four dropping pipettes • wooden splint • permanent marker pen • three stopwatches • two 10 cm³ measuring cylinders • test-tube rack • glass or plastic stirring rod

Access to:

• ethanol • 0.100 mol dm⁻³ silver nitrate solution • 1-chlorobutane, 2-chlorobutane and 2-chloro-2-methylpropane • boiling water (ideally a kettle)

Safety considerations

- Make sure you have read the advice in the Safety section at the beginning of this book and listen to any advice from your teacher before carrying out this investigation.

- The ethanol is flammable and should be kept away from any naked flames.

- The halogenoalkanes are flammable and harmful.

- The silver nitrate is an irritant and is harmful. It can also cause skin discolouration.

Part 1: Preparation of the reaction mixtures

Method

1 You will need three test tubes for the silver nitrate solution and three for the ethanol and halogenoalkane.

2 Using the permanent marker pen, label the test tubes appropriately. Near the bottom of the wooden splint, draw a cross using either a pencil or the marker pen.

3 **a** Add 2 cm³ of silver nitrate solution to three of the test tubes.

   b Add 2 cm³ of ethanol to the remaining three. Make sure your additions match the labels.

4 Place stoppers in the three tubes used for the ethanol.

Results

Draw up an appropriate results table in the space provided.

Table 9.2

Data analysis

a Explain the function of the following:

   i Silver nitrate solution. Include any relevant equations in your answer.

   ....

   ....

   ....

   ....

   ....

ii Ethanol

....

....

....

....

....

Part 2: Carrying out the reactions

Method

5 Half-fill the 250 cm³ beaker with boiling water and then add cold water so that the temperature is approximately 50–55 °C.

6 Add five drops of each of the three halogenoalkanes to the appropriately labelled ethanol test tube and stopper the tubes. See Figure 9.2.

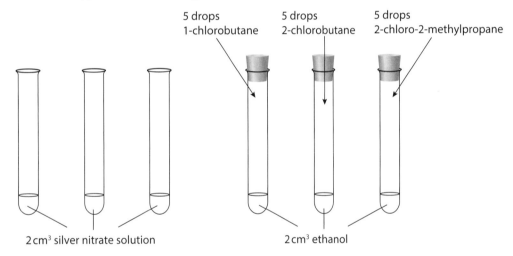

Figure 9.2

7 Place all six test tubes in the beaker and leave for about 5 min so that they are at the same temperature as the water in the beaker.

8 a Quickly mix the silver nitrate and ethanol tubes for the primary halogenoalkane and start one of the stopwatches.

   b After 1 min, repeat for the secondary halogenoalkane and start the second stopwatch.

c Carry out the process for the tertiary halogenoalkane. Figure 9.3 shows the apparatus set-up.

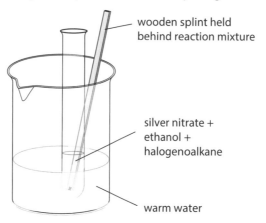

Figure 9.3

9 Time how long it takes for the reaction to be completed for each halogenoalkane. Then calculate the rate for each halogenoalkane and record it in Table 9.2.

Data analysis

b Explain how you decided when the reaction had finished in Step 9.

....

....

....

c Explain how you calculated the rate for each halogenoalkane.

....

....

d Calculate the relative rates for the three halogenoalkanes.

....

....

....

....

....

e Name the mechanism by which each halogenoalkane undergoes hydrolysis and use these facts to explain the relative rates for their hydrolysis.

....

....

....

....

....

....

....

....

....

....

....

....

Evaluation

f Identify sources of error in this experiment.

....

....

....

....

g Draw up a table that lists the control variables in the experiment and for each one describe why they are kept constant.

Chapter outline

This chapter relates to Chapter 17: Alcohols, esters and carboxylic acids and Chapter 18: Carbonyl compounds in the coursebook.

In this chapter you will complete an investigation on:

- 10.1 Identifying four unknown organic compounds

Practical investigation 10.1:
Identifying four unknown organic compounds

Introduction

In this practical, you will observe Part 1, then complete Parts 2 and 3 in order to identify the functional groups in four unknown organic compounds P, Q, R and S containing oxygen. Note: each of the four compounds contain three carbon atoms.

Part 1: Test for hydroxyl groups using phosphorus pentachloride

This part of the investigation is an observed demonstration

Safety considerations

- Make sure you have read the advice in the Safety section at the beginning of this book and listen to any advice from your teacher before carrying out this investigation.

- The demonstration must take place in a fume cupboard.

- You must wear eye protection and tie long hair back.

- Ensure that you stand at least two metres away from the fume cupboard during the demonstration.

Method

The apparatus set-up for the demonstration is shown in Figure 10.1

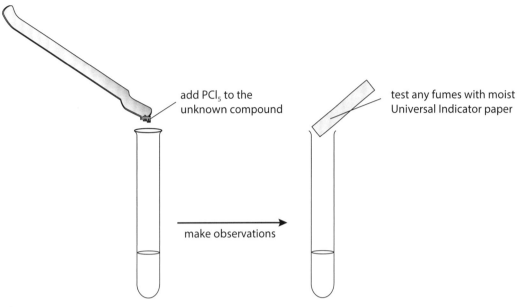

add PCl_5 to the unknown compound

make observations

test any fumes with moist Universal Indicator paper

Figure 10.1

Results

Complete Table 10.1 with your observations.

Unknown compound	Observations
P	
Q	
R	
S	

Table 10.1

Data analysis

a What do your observations (Table 10.1) tell you about the four unknown compounds?

....

....

Evaluation

b Explain your conclusions. Include relevant equations.

....

....

Before proceeding with the investigation, clearly identify and label which of the unknown compounds do and do not contain a hydroxyl group after observing Part 1.

Record your identifications in the space provided.

....

....

....

....

Part 2: Investigating the compounds that **do** contain a hydroxyl group

Equipment

You will need:

- six test tubes • test-tube rack • Bunsen burner and heat-resistant pad • wooden splint
- spatula • two evaporating basins • graduated droppers • 250 cm^3 glass beaker

Access to:

- samples of the unknown compounds that tested positive for a hydroxyl group in Part 1
- sodium hydrogen carbonate • sodium carbonate solution • 2.00 mol dm^{-3} sodium hydroxide solution • limewater solution • wash bottle filled with distilled water
- concentrated sulfuric acid in a dropper bottle • porcelain dish or a white tile • glacial ethanoic acid • hot water (kettle) • iodine solution

Safety considerations

- Make sure you have read the advice in the Safety section at the beginning of this book and listen to any advice from your teacher before carrying out this investigation.

- Eye protection must be worn at all times and tie long hair back.

- The limewater is an alkali and should be treated as corrosive.

- Sodium hydroxide solution is corrosive.

- The organic compounds are flammable and must be kept away from naked flames.

- The organic compounds must also be regarded as being harmful. If possible, plastic gloves should be worn to minimise contact.

- The concentrated sulfuric acid is corrosive. Always add concentrated sulfuric acid to water **never** the other way around. If you get any acid on your skin, wash off immediately using large amounts of cold water.

- Hot water should be provided by a kettle.

- The product of the reaction in Part 2c is strongly irritating to eyes. As soon as you have made your observations, wash the reaction mixture down the sink with plenty of water.

- The iodine solution will stain the skin so handle with care.

Part 2a: Test for carboxylic acid group

Method

1 For each unknown compound that tested positive for a hydroxyl group in Part 1, complete the procedures shown in Figure 10.2. You will need to set up two test tubes per compound tested as shown.

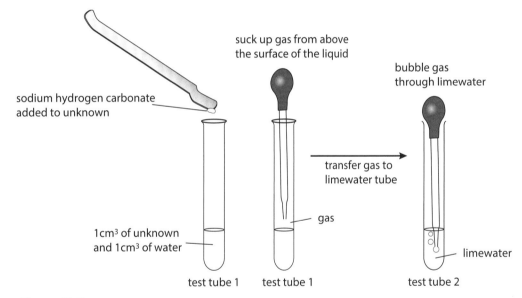

sodium hydrogen carbonate added to unknown

suck up gas from above the surface of the liquid

bubble gas through limewater

transfer gas to limewater tube

gas

1cm³ of unknown and 1cm³ of water

limewater

test tube 1   test tube 1   test tube 2

Figure 10.2

2 Prepare a table (Table 10.2) and record your observations.

Results

Create and complete Table 10.2 in the space provided.

Table 10.2

Data analysis

c   Which of the unknown compounds contain a carboxylic acid group?

....

d   Explain your answer.

....

....

e   Identify this compound and give the equation for the reaction taking place.

....

....

....

Part 2b: Test for the alcohol (R–OH) group

Method

1   For the compound that tested positive for a hydroxyl group in Part 1 but tested negative for a carboxyl group in Part 2a, complete the procedures shown in Figure 10.3.

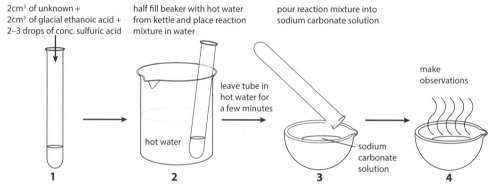

Figure 10.3

Results

Record your observations in the space provided.

....

....

....

....

....

....

Data analysis

f What has been formed in this reaction?

....

g Give the TWO possible identities of the unknown compound and explain your answer.

....

....

....

Part 2c: Iodoform reaction: test for CH$_3$CH(OH)– group or the CH$_3$CO– group

The iodoform reaction is used to identify either the CH$_3$CH(OH)– group or the CH$_3$CO– group. These groups react with IO$^-$ ions to form a yellow precipitate of iodoform (CHI$_3$). Using this test will enable you to identify the compound tested in Part 2b.

Method

1 Add five drops of the unknown compound to a test tube.

2 Add five drops of iodine solution.

3 Add sodium hydroxide solution drop by drop until the brown colour of the iodine just disappears.

Results

Describe your observations.

....

....

Data analysis

h Identify the organic compound and explain your answer.

....

....

....

....

HINT
Remember it
contains three
carbons

111

Part 3: Identifying the compounds that do **not** contain the hydroxyl group

Equipment

You will need:

• two test tubes • three graduated droppers • permanent marker pen • 1 very clean (new if possible) test tube for Tollens test.

Access to:

• 2,4-di-nitrophenylhydrazine (2,4-DNPH or Brady's reagent) solution in methanol
• 1 250cm³ beaker; 0.10 mol dm⁻³ silver nitrate solution; 2.0 mol dm⁻³ sodium hydroxide solution
• fresh 2 mol dm⁻³ ammonia solution.
• Hot water or a kettle.

Safety considerations

- Make sure you have read the advice in the Safety section at the beginning of this book and listen to any advice from your teacher before carrying out this investigation.

- 2,4-DNPH and the methanol it is dissolved in are toxic. Methanol is also flammable

- Eye protection must be worn at all times and tie long hair back.

Part 3a: Reaction with 2,4-di-nitrophenylhydrazine

Method

1 Add five drops of the unknown compound in a test tube.

2 Add 5 cm³ of 2,4-DNPH and record your observations in the space provided.

3 Repeat Steps 1 and 2 with the other unknown compound that does not contain the hydroxyl group.

Results

Record your observations in the space provided.

....

....

Data analysis

i Explain your observations.

....

Part 3b: Reaction with Tollens' reagent

Method

1 Complete the procedures shown in Figure 10.4 for both unknown compounds.

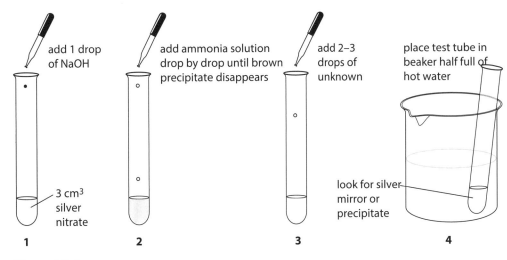

Figure 10.4

Results

Record your observations in the space provided.

....

....

Data analysis

j Using your results, identify the two unknown compounds and explain your answers.

....

....

....

....

Evaluation

k The four unknown compounds are:

P = ...

Q = ...

R = ...

S = ...

Chapter 11

More about enthalpy changes

Chapter outline

This chapter relates to Chapter 4: Chemical bonding, Chapter 6: Enthalpy changes and Chapter 19: Lattice energy in the coursebook.

In this chapter you will complete investigations on:

- 11.1 Enthalpy change of vaporisation of water
- 11.2 Enthalpy change of solution of chlorides
- 11.3 Thermal decomposition of iron(II) ethanedioate
- 11.4 Thermal decomposition of metal carbonates
- 11.5 Enthalpy change of mixing

Practical investigation 11.1:
Enthalpy change of vaporisation of water

Extension investigation

Introduction

The enthalpy change of vaporisation is the energy required to vaporise one mole of liquid at its boiling point at a pressure of one atmosphere. This value can be determined by measuring the energy required to heat up and then boil away a particular mass of water.

Equipment

You will need:

- clamp stand, two clamps and two bosses • Bunsen burner • conical flask, 500 cm³
- measuring cylinder, 100 cm³ or 250 cm³ • long-stemmed thermometer, 0–100 °C • cork or rubber bung with hole bored to fit thermometer • stopclock or stopwatch • glass rod or wire loop for stirring

Access to:

- distilled water • means of lighting the Bunsen burner

Safety considerations

- Make sure you have read the advice in the Safety section at the beginning of this book and listen to any advice from your teacher before carrying out this investigation.

- The steam produced can cause burns.

Method

1   Use the measuring cylinder to put 200 cm³ distilled water into the conical flask.

2   Set up the apparatus as shown in Figure 11.1 with the Bunsen burner unlit.

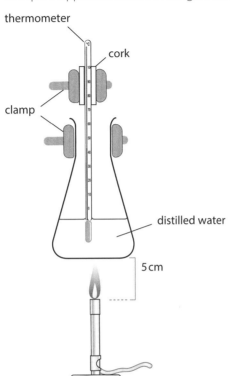

thermometer

cork

clamp

distilled water

5 cm

Figure 11.1

3   Move the Bunsen burner from under the flask and light it so that a blue flame is produced which is just under 5 cm high.

4   Put the Bunsen burner under the flask so that the tip of the flame is in the centre of the flask but not quite touching the flask. Immediately start the stopclock and read the thermometer. Record this in Table 11.1

5   Keep the water in the flask stirred and record the temperature of the water in Table 11.1 every 30 s until the water boils.

6   Continue boiling the water for exactly 10 minutes, recording the temperature every 2 minutes.

7   Turn off the Bunsen burner and allow the water to cool.

8   Measure the volume of the water that remains in the flask.

! HINT
Make sure that the top of the Bunsen burner is 5 cm from the bottom of the flask and that the thermometer does not touch the bottom of the flask

! HINT
Make sure that:
- the tip of the Bunsen flame does not quite touch the bottom of the flask
- you do not alter this flame for the rest of the experiment.

Results

Construct a table of results in the space provided.

Table 11.1

Data analysis

a On the grid provided, plot a graph of temperature against time.

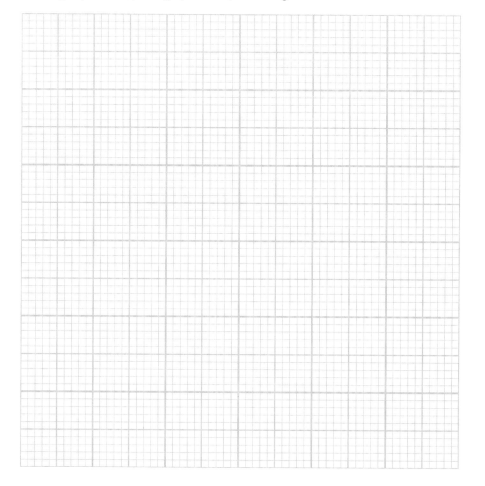

b From your graph, calculate the rate of temperature rise, in °C / minute, until the water is boiling.

………

c Calculate the energy supplied by the flame per minute. Note: specific thermal capacity of water = 4.18 J g^{-1} °C^{-1}.

> **HINT**
> Remember that energy = mass × specific thermal capacity × temperature rise

Energy/min = ………………… J min^{-1}

d Calculate the energy supplied by the flame during the 10 minutes that the water was boiling.

Energy = ………………… J

e Calculate the number of moles of water converted to steam.

= ………………… mol

f Calculate the energy required to change one mole of water at its boiling point to steam.

= ………………… J mol^{-1}

Evaluation

g Why should the thermometer not touch the bottom of the flask?

………

………

h What assumptions have been made in the calculations?

………

………

i Compare your result with the actual value of the enthalpy change of vaporisation of 40.65 kJ mol^{-1}. Apart from random errors, suggest why your value is likely to be higher.

....

....

....

j Refer to the equipment used to suggest how the accuracy of the experiment could be improved.

....

....

....

k Apart from errors in measurements, suggest two other sources of error in this experiment and how these errors can be minimised.

....

....

....

....

l Why must you not use this method to find the enthalpy change of vaporisation of ethanol?

....

....

m Suggest a different method of heating the water to its boiling point?

....

....

Practical investigation 11.2:
Enthalpy change of solution of chlorides

Introduction

The enthalpy change of solution is the energy absorbed or released when one mole of a solid dissolves in water to form a very dilute solution. This value can be determined by measuring the temperature change when a known amount of solute is added to a fixed amount of water.

Equipment

You will need:

• expanded polystyrene cup and beaker, 250 cm³ • lid with hole for thermometer to fit the polystyrene cup • measuring cylinder, 20 cm³ (or 10 cm³) • thermometer, −10–100 °C (preferably with 0.1 °C graduations)

Access to:

• Distilled water • Balance to weigh to at least 1 decimal place • Weighing boats
• Anhydrous lithium chloride in stoppered container with spatula • Anhydrous sodium chloride in stoppered container with spatula • Anhydrous potassium chloride in stoppered container with spatula • Anhydrous magnesium chloride in stoppered container with spatula
• Anhydrous calcium chloride in stoppered container with spatula

Safety considerations

- Make sure you have read the advice in the Safety section at the beginning of this book and listen to any advice from your teacher before carrying out this investigation.

- Anhydrous calcium chloride is an irritant. The other chlorides are low hazard.

Method

1 Weigh out 1.7 g of lithium chloride as accurately as possible.

2 Use the measuring cylinder to pour 20 cm3 of distilled water into the polystyrene cup (see Figure 11.2).

3 Record the temperature of the water in the polystyrene cup every 30 seconds for two minutes.

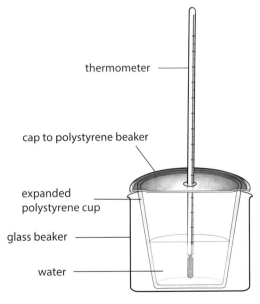

thermometer

cap to polystyrene beaker

expanded polystyrene cup

glass beaker

water

Figure 11.2

4   After two and a half minutes, add the lithium chloride to the water and stir the solution with the thermometer.

5   Record the temperature of the solution in the polystyrene cup every 30 seconds, with continuous stirring, for at least another 2 minutes.

6   Wash the polystyrene cup with distilled water and dry it.

7   Repeat steps 1 to 6 using but this time using 2.3 g of sodium chloride.

8   Repeat steps 1 to 6 using but this time using 3.0 g of potassium chloride.

9   Repeat steps 1 to 6 using but this time using 3.8 g of magnesium chloride.

10 Repeat steps 1 to 6 using but this time using 4.4 g of calcium chloride.

Results

Construct a table of results in the space provided.

Data Analysis

a   For each chloride determine the maximum temperature change when it dissolves in water and enter your results into Table 11.2.

Chloride	Maximum temperature change
LiCl	
NaCl	
KCl	
$MgCl_2$	
$CaCl_2$	

Table 11.2

HINT

See Skills chapter for the method of determining a corrected temperature change

b For potassium chloride only, plot a graph of corrected temperature against time and extrapolate the straight-line portion of the graph to determine the corrected temperature change.

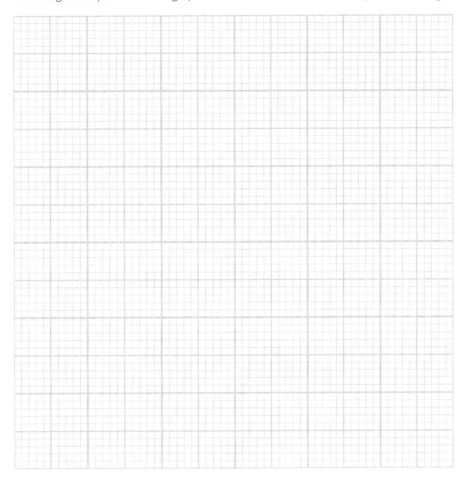

c For potassium chloride, calculate the energy change in joules stating any assumptions that you have made.

Note: specific thermal capacity of water = 4.18 J g^{-1} °C^{-1})

Energy change = ... J

d The same number of moles of each chloride was used (0.04 moles).

Calculate the enthalpy change of solution of potassium chloride from the quantity of salt present and energy change calculated in part **c**.

= .... J mol^{-1}

e Comment on the relationship between the enthalpy change of solution and the position of the chlorides in Group I.

....

....

f Comment on the relationship between the enthalpy change of solution and the position of the chlorides in Periods 3 and 4.

....

....

Evaluation

g Why was a series of temperature readings taken at different times rather than just two readings: the initial temperature of the water and the greatest temperature change?

....

....

h Refer to the equipment used to suggest how the accuracy of the experiment could be improved.

....

....

....

i Suggest how to improve the method to take into account the initial temperature of the solid.

....

....

j Refer to the definition of enthalpy change of solution in the introduction to this experiment to suggest why your value is likely to be lower than the actual value.

....

....

....

Practical investigation 11.3: Planning
Thermal decomposition of iron(II) ethanedioate

Introduction

Iron(II) ethanedioate, $Fe(COO)_2$, is an ionic compound which decomposes when heated to form iron(II) oxide, carbon monoxide and carbon dioxide.

$$Fe(COO)_2(s) \rightarrow FeO(s) + CO(g) + CO_2(g)$$

You are going to plan a single experiment to show that the molar ratio of iron(II) oxide and carbon monoxide produced agrees with the equation shown.

The following information will be useful in answering the questions in the Data analysis and Evaluation sections:

- The solubility of carbon monoxide in water is 2.14×10^{-4} mol dm^{-3}

- Carbon monoxide does not react with aqueous alkalis unless heated under pressure

- Carbon monoxide is very poisonous

- The solubility of carbon dioxide in water is 3.29×10^{-2} mol dm^{-3}

- Carbon dioxide is a slightly acidic gas that reacts with aqueous alkalis

- Iron(II) ethanedioate is poisonous

Equipment

You are provided with anhydrous iron(II) ethanedioate and have access to common laboratory equipment and reagents. The equipment needs to be capable of absorbing carbon dioxide and collecting carbon monoxide.

List the equipment and any additional chemicals required.

- ....
- ....
- ....
- ....

- ....
- ....
- ....
- ....

Safety considerations

- What precautions would you take to make sure that the experiment is performed safely?

....

....

....

Method

- Draw a labelled diagram to show the arrangement of the apparatus.

- Describe how you would carry out the experiment.

1 ....
....

2 ....
....

3 ....
....

4 ....
....

5 ....
....
....
....

Data analysis

a State the maximum volume of the piece of equipment that you used to collect the gas.

....

b State an appropriate volume of carbon monoxide that should be collected in the gas collector.

....

HINT

One mole of any gas occupies 24.0 dm³ at room temperature and pressure

c   Calculate the number of moles of carbon monoxide present in the volume you chose for part **b**.

= .... mol

d   Calculate the mass of iron(II) ethanedioate that needs to be heated to produce the number of moles of carbon monoxide you calculated in part **c**.

= .... g

HINT

You need to refer to the equation at the start of the investigation:
C = 12.0, Fe = 55.8, O = 16.0

e   Explain how you would use the results of the experiment to show that the decomposition had occurred according to the molar ratio of iron(II) oxide : carbon monoxide shown in the equation.

....

....

....

....

Evaluation

f   How could you make sure that the iron(II) ethanedioate had completely decomposed?

....

....

g   What should you do before collecting the gas to make sure that the gas measurement is accurate?

....

....

h   Suggest how, and explain to what extent, the procedure that you used is likely to be effective.

....

....

....

Practical investigation 11.4: Planning
Thermal decomposition of metal carbonates

Introduction

Some metal carbonates decompose easily when heated, while for others the decomposition is more difficult. A metal oxide and carbon dioxide are formed.

You are going to plan an experiment to compare the ease with which four metal carbonates decompose using a method which does **not** involve the collection of a gas. The carbonates are copper(II) carbonate, iron(II) carbonate, lead(II) carbonate, magnesium carbonate and sodium carbonate.

The following information will be useful in answering the questions in the Data analysis and Evaluation sections:

- Copper(II) carbonate is harmful. It is generally sold as basic copper carbonate which also contains copper(II) hydroxide.

- Iron(II) carbonate is low hazard. It oxidises readily in air to form iron(III) compounds .

- Lead(II) carbonate is toxic.

- Magnesium carbonate and sodium carbonate are low hazard.

- A cloudy white precipitate is formed when carbon dioxide reacts with an aqueous solution of calcium hydroxide. The precipitate dissolves when carbon dioxide is in excess.

- Calcium hydroxide is an irritant as a solid.

Equipment

You are provided with samples of each of the carbonates as well as solid calcium hydroxide. You have access to common laboratory equipment.

List the equipment required.

- ………………………………………………………..
- ………………………………………………………..
- ………………………………………………………..
- ………………………………………………………..

- …………………………………………………………
- …………………………………………………………
- …………………………………………………………
- …………………………………………………………

Safety considerations

What precautions would you take to make sure that the experiment is performed safely?

………..

………..

………..

………..

Method

- Describe how you would prepare a saturated solution of calcium hydroxide.

....

....

....

- Draw a labelled diagram to show the arrangement of the apparatus.

- Describe how you would carry out the experiment.

HINT

How will you compare the amount of each carbonate used so that the experiment is a fair test?

1 ....

....

2 ....

....

3 ....

....

....

....

....

....

4 ....

....

5 ....

....

....

....

Data analysis

a The solubility of calcium hydroxide in water is 1.53×10^{-2} mol dm^{-3}.

Calculate the minimum volume of solid calcium hydroxide needed to produce 100 cm^3 of a saturated solution of calcium hydroxide. (A_r values: Ca = 40.1, H = 1.0, O = 16.0)

= .... g

b Identify two variables, other than the amount of solid, which should be controlled in this experiment and give a reason why they should be controlled.

....

....

....

....

c Draw a table of results which can be used to record and process the data from this experiment assuming that the whole experiment was repeated once more. You do not have to fill in the table.

d The results of this experiment can be very variable. Draw another results table to show the results in a qualitative manner in terms of ease of decomposition.

Evaluation

e What is the main source of error which limits an accurate assessment of the relative ease of decomposition in this experiment compared with a method involving the measurement of the volume of carbon dioxide?

....

....

f Why must the delivery tube be removed from the limewater as soon as heating is stopped?

....

....

g To what extent is the procedure that you used likely to give accurate and consistent results? Give reasons for your answer.

....

....

....

....

....

....

....

....

HINT
Some of the information in the introduction section will be useful

Practical investigation 11.5: Data analysis
Enthalpy change of mixing

Introduction

When two different liquids mix, there is sometimes an enthalpy change. The enthalpy change is due to a change in the type of intermolecular forces between the molecules.

Two liquids, trichloromethane ($CHCl_3$) and methanol (CH_3OH) were mixed in different proportions using two $100\,cm^3$ measuring cylinders, one for each liquid. Each mixture was stirred and the temperature change recorded using a thermometer accurate to the nearest $0.1\,°C$. The total volume of the liquids was always $60\,cm^3$. The experiment was repeated (second run).

The following information will be useful in answering some of the questions:

- Trichloromethane is harmful. Its boiling point is $62\,°C$.

- Methanol is highly flammable and toxic. Its boiling point is $65\,°C$.

You are going to analyse the data provided, evaluate the experiment and interpret the results.

Safety

What precautions would you take to make sure that the experiment is performed safely?

....

....

....

Results

Volume of $CHCl_3$ / cm^3	Volume of CH_3OH / cm^3	Increase in temperature (first run) / °C	Increase in temperature (second run) / °C	Average increase in temperature / °C
0	60	0	0	
5	55	0.3	0.5	
10	50	0.9	0.7	
15	45	1.0	1.4	
20	40	1.1	1.4	
25	35	2.0	2.0	
30	30	2.1	2.6	
35	25	2.7	2.6	
40	20	2.9	2.7	
45	15	2.7	2.6	
50	10	1.8	2.3	
55	5	1.2	0.8	
60	0	0	0	

Table 11.3

Data analysis

a Complete the last column in Table 11.3.

b Identify the dependent and independent variables in this investigation.

Dependent variable ....

Independent variable ....

c On the grid, plot a graph to show how the temperature changes when the two solutions are mixed in different proportions. Draw the curve of best fit.

....

HINT
For one of the axes you can use either the volume of CHCl$_3$ or the volume of CH$_3$OH.

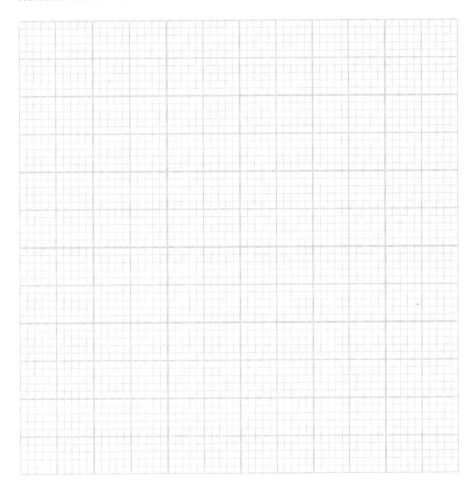

d Deduce the volume of trichloromethane and methane present when the increase in temperature was the greatest.

....

e Calculate the mass of both trichloromethane and methane present at this temperature.

(densities: trichloromethane, 1.47 g cm^{-3}, methanol, 0.79 g cm^{-3})

f   Calculate the number of moles of both trichloromethane and methane present at this temperature. A_r values: C = 12.0, Cl = 35.5, H = 1.0, O = 16.0

g   Use your answer to part **f** and your knowledge of intermolecular forces to explain the shape of the graph.

....

....

....

....

Evaluation

h   The table does not show all the data collected.

What data are missing from the table and why is it important that this data be included?

....

....

....

i   Which point on the graph is anomalous and how did you deal with this point?

....

....

j   Comment on the range and reproducibility of the data and suggest what you would do to get more reliable results.

....

....

....

....

....

k   State and explain two possible sources of error in this experiment.

....

....

....

Chapter 12:
Electrochemistry

Chapter outline

This chapter relates to Chapter 20: Electrochemistry in the coursebook.

In this chapter you will complete investigations on:

- 12.1 Determining the Faraday constant
- 12.2 Comparing the voltage of electrochemical cells
- 12.3 Half-cells containing only ions as reactants
- 12.4 Changing the concentration of ions in an electrochemical cell
- 12.5 The electrical conductivity of ethanoic aid

Practical investigation 12.1:
Determining the Faraday constant

Introduction

The amount of electrical charge carried by one mole of electrons is called the Faraday constant.

This value can be determined by measuring the gain in mass of a copper cathode when passing an electric current for a known time interval during the electrolysis of aqueous of copper(II) sulfate.

Equipment

You will need:

- ammeter, 0–1 A • variable resistor, 100 Ohms • 6V power pack or battery pack • electrical on–off switch • five connecting wires • glass beaker, 150 cm³ • cardboard electrode holder • 0.5 mol dm⁻³ copper(II) sulfate solution, 100 cm³ • two copper foils 6 cm × 2 cm (for use as electrodes) • two crocodile clips • clock or watch to record to 45 minutes • plastic gloves

Access to:

- distilled water in wash bottle • 2 mol dm⁻³ nitric acid • ethanol • tweezers or clean tongs • drying oven set at 100 °C • balance to weigh to at least two decimal places

---

Safety considerations

- Make sure you have read the advice in the Safety section at the beginning of this book and listen to any advice from your teacher before carrying out this investigation.

- Wear eye protection throughout.

- Copper(II) sulfate is harmful.

- Dilute nitric acid is an irritant.

- Ethanol is highly flammable.

- The edges of the metal foils are sharp: handle them with care.

Method

1 Using tongs or tweezers, dip each copper electrode into 2 mol dm⁻³ nitric acid for about 20 s.

2 Rinse each electrode with distilled water.

3 Rinse each electrode with ethanol.

4 Dry each electrode in a drying oven at 100 °C.

5 Allow the electrodes to cool.

6 Accurately weigh the electrode which is to be the cathode (to two decimal places). Record this mass in the Results section.

7 Arrange the apparatus as shown in Figure 12.1(a), leaving the switch open and the variable resistor at maximum resistance.

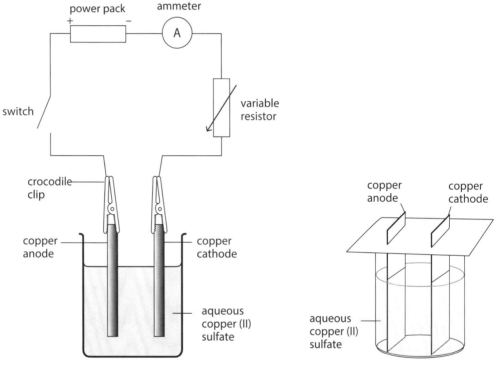

Figure 12.1a   **Figure 12.1b**

8 Pour 100 cm³ of aqueous copper(II) sulfate into the beaker and arrange the copper electrodes as shown in Figure 12.1(b). **Make sure that you know which electrode is the cathode**.

9 When everything is ready, note the exact time, close the electrical switch and quickly adjust the variable resistor so that the reading on the ammeter is 0.2 A.

10 Keep the electric current at 0.2 A throughout the experiment by adjusting the variable resistor.

11 Record any observations in the Results section.

12 After exactly 45 minutes, switch off the current.

13 Carefully remove the cathode and rinse it with distilled water and then with ethanol.

14 Dry the cathode as before. Allow it to cool and then reweigh it. Record your results.

HINT

Observations may include any colour changes or changes taking place around the electrodes

134

Results

Mass of cathode at the start of the experiment .... g

Mass of cathode at the end of the experiment .... g

Gain in mass of the cathode .... g

Average current passed .... A

Time .... s

Other observations

....

....

Data analysis

a   Use the relationship $Q = It$ (where Q is charge in coulombs, C, I is current in amps and t is seconds) to calculate the charge passing during the experiment.

charge = ... C

b   Calculate the number of moles of copper deposited. (A_r : Cu = 63.5)

.... mol

c   The equation for the reaction at the cathode is: $Cu^{2+}(aq) + 2e^- \rightarrow Cu(s)$

How many moles of electrons are required to deposit one mole of copper?

.... mol

d   Calculate the charge on one mole of electrons (Faraday constant).

.... C

e   What observations did you make at the electrodes?

....

....

Evaluation

f Compare your result with the actual value of the Faraday constant (96 500 C mol⁻¹).

The value is often higher than the actual value. Apart from random errors suggest why this value is likely to be higher.

....

....

....

g A weighing error was made. The mass of the cathode at the start of the experiment was higher than the actual mass. What effect would this have on the value of the Faraday constant? Explain your reasoning.

....

....

....

h Why were the electrodes washed in nitric acid and then with ethanol?

....

....

i Apart from weighing errors, suggest three other errors that could contribute to an incorrect value of the Faraday constant in this experiment. Include one example of another variable that needs to be controlled.

....

....

....

j Suggest why it is better to measure the mass loss of the anode rather than the gain in mass of the cathode.

....

....

Practical investigation 12.2:
Comparing the voltage of electrochemical cells

Introduction

When zinc reacts with copper(II) ions, energy is released as heat. Electrons are transferred from zinc to the copper(II) ions. If the zinc atoms are kept apart from the copper(II) ions by setting up an electrochemical cell, the electrons can be made to flow through a wire and a voltage is produced. This voltage is called the cell potential, E_{cell}. You are first going to investigate the reactions between zinc and copper(II) ions, zinc and iron(II) ions, and iron and copper(II) ions.

Equipment
You will need:

• high resistance voltmeter • three beakers, 100 cm³ • two connecting wires • two crocodile clips • three strips of filter paper 10 cm × 1 cm soaked with saturated potassium nitrate solution • emery paper (or sandpaper) • iron nail • zinc foil, 6 cm × 2 cm • copper foil, 6 cm × 2 cm • 1.0 mol dm⁻³ aqueous copper(II) sulfate, 50 cm³ • 1.0 mol dm⁻³ aqueous zinc sulfate, 50 cm³ • 1.0 mol dm⁻³ aqueous acidified iron(II) sulfate, 50 cm³ • gloves

Access to:

• distilled water in a wash bottle and paper towels

Safety considerations

- Make sure you have read the advice in the Safety section at the beginning of this book and listen to any advice from your teacher before carrying out this investigation.

- mol dm⁻³ aqueous copper(II) sulfate is harmful if swallowed. It is also an irritant.

- mol dm⁻³ aqueous zinc(II) sulfate is harmful if swallowed. It is also an irritant.

- mol dm⁻³ aqueous iron(II) sulfate is harmful if swallowed. It is also an irritant.

- Take care not to raise metal dust when cleaning the electrodes.

- Aqueous potassium nitrate solution is low hazard but the solid is oxidising.

Method

1 Clean the strips of zinc and copper and the iron nail with emery paper or sandpaper.

2 Place 50 cm³ of zinc sulfate in one beaker and 50 cm³ of copper(II) sulfate solution in another.

3 Connect the two half-cells with a salt bridge made from a strip of filter paper soaked in potassium nitrate solution as shown in Figure 12.2.

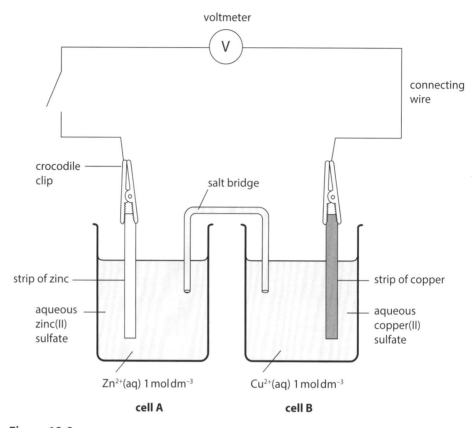

Figure 12.2

4 Connect the strips of copper and zinc to the external circuit as shown above (Cell A)

5 Record the steady voltage on the voltmeter.

6 Remove the strips of zinc and copper and wash them with distilled water then dry them with a paper towel.

7 Repeat the experiment using zinc dipping into zinc sulfate and iron dipping into iron(II) sulfate. Use a fresh salt bridge (Cell B).

8 Repeat the experiment using copper dipping into copper sulfate and iron dipping into iron(II) sulfate. Use a fresh salt bridge (Cell C).

Results

Cell A Voltage of zinc / copper cell, E_{cell} V

Cell B Voltage of zinc / iron cell, E_{cell} V

Cell C Voltage of iron / copper cell, E_{cell} V

Data analysis

a Use the voltages of Cells A and B to predict the voltage of Cell C

HINT
- The half-cell is a metal dipping into a solution of its ions
- The half-cell which is the negative pole has the metal which releases electrons better

b Predict the polarity of each half-cell for:

Cell A ....

Cell B ....

Cell C ....

c Which metal is the best reducing agent? Explain your answer?

....

Evaluation

d Why were the strips of metal cleaned with emery paper or sandpaper?

....

e Why was a fresh salt bridge used for each of Cells A, B and C?

....

f How did the predicted value for the voltage of Cell C compare with your experimental value? Suggest reasons for any difference.

....

....

....

g The standard electrode potential, E°_{cell}, for cell C is 0.73 V.

Explain why the value measured in your experiment, E_{cell}, is not the standard electrode potential.

....

....

Practical investigation 12.3:
Half-cells containing only ions as reactants

Introduction

The reaction between aqueous iron(III) ions and aqueous iodide ions is a redox reaction. You are going to investigate the products of this reaction in a preliminary experiment. In Investigation 12.4 you will then plan a design for an electrochemical cell in which this reaction can take place so that a standard cell potential can be measured.

The following information will be useful:

- starch solution reacts with iodine to give a blue/black solution

- potassium hexacyanoferrate(III) reacts with $Fe^{2+}(aq)$ to give a dark blue solution

Equipment for preliminary experiment

You will need:

• six test tubes in a test-tube rack • dropping pipettes • beaker for distilled water to wash pipettes if needed

Access to:

• distilled water • 0.1 mol dm^{-3} aqueous ammonium iron(III) sulfate (iron alum) • 0.1 mol dm^{-3} aqueous potassium iodide • 1% starch solution in a small bottle with a dropping pipette • 1% aqueous potassium hexacyanoferrate(III) in a small bottle with a dropping pipette

Safety considerations

• Make sure you have read the advice in the Safety section at the beginning of this book and listen to any advice from your teacher before carrying out this investigation.

• At the concentrations used all the solutions are low risk although potassium hexacyanoferrate(III) may cause eye irritation and skin irritation.

Method

1 Use a dropping pipette to put about 2 cm^3 of ammonium iron(III) sulfate solution into the test tube then add a few drops of starch solution. Record your observations in Table 12.1.

2 Take a new test tube and add about 2 cm^3 of ammonium iron(III) sulfate solution followed by a few drops of potassium hexacyanoferrate(III) solution. Record your observations in Table 12.1.

3 Take a new test tube and add about 2 cm^3 of potassium iodide solution followed by a few drops of starch solution. Record your observations in Table 12.1.

4 Take a new test tube and add about 2 cm^3 of potassium iodide solution followed by a few drops of potassium hexacyanoferrate(III) solution. Record your observations in Table 12.1.

5 To a new test tube, add about 2 cm^3 of ammonium iron(III) sulfate solution.

6 Add an equal volume of potassium iodide solution to the ammonium iron(III) sulfate solution. Record your observations in Table 12.1.

7 Pour half the contents of the test tube into a clean test tube.

8 To one of the test tubes, add a few drops of starch solution. Record your observations in Table 12.1.

9 To the other test tube, add a few drops of potassium hexacyanoferrate(III) solution. Record your observations in Table 12.1.

Results

Record the results for each step in Table 12.1

Step 1	
Step 2	
Step 3	
Step 4	
Step 6	
Step 8	
Step 9	

Table 12.1

Data analysis

a Give the names and formulae of the ion and molecule formed in the reaction in Step 6.

....

> **HINT**
> Use the information in the introduction and the results of Steps 1-4 to help you

b Construct the two half equations for the reaction in Step 6.

....

....

c Construct a full ionic equation for the reaction in Step 6.

....

> **HINT**
> You will need to consider both the oxidised and reduced forms of the species present in the solution in each half-cell

d Comment about the relative oxidising and reducing abilities of each reactant?

....

....

e This reaction can be used to produce a voltage in an electrochemical cell. Draw a diagram of the electrochemical cell in which this reaction can take place so that a voltage is produced. Label your diagram fully.

141

Evaluation

f What was the purpose of Steps 1–4 in the Method section?

....

....

g State two conditions required if you were designing the electrochemical cell in part **d** for measuring the standard cell potential.

....

....

Practical investigation 12.4: Planning
Changing the concentration of ions in an electrochemical cell

Introduction

The concentration of an ion in an electrochemical half-cell affects the value of E_{cell}. You are to plan an experiment to demonstrate how the value of E_{cell} varies in a cell made up of a Zn/Zn^{2+} half-cell and a Cu/Cu^{2+} half-cell.

Equipment

You are provided with solutions of $1.0 \ mol \ dm^{-3}$ aqueous copper(II) sulfate and $1.0 \ mol \ dm^{-3}$ aqueous zinc sulfate. You also have access to common laboratory equipment and reagents.

List the equipment and any additional substances required.

- ....
- ....
- ....
- ....
- ....
- ....

- ....
- ....
- ....
- ....
- ....
- ....

Method

Describe how you would carry out the experiment.

....

....

....

....

....

....

Results

The effect of concentration on the standard electrode potential for a metal / metal ion reaction is described by the relationship:

$$E = E° + \frac{0.59}{z} \log [\text{ion}]$$

E is the electrode potential at non-standard concentrations, $E°$ is the standard electrode potential, z is the number of electrons transferred.

Draw a results table to include the concentration of the ion, $\log [Cu^{2+}]$, and E_{cell}.

Data analysis

a Which is the dependent variable and which is the independent variable in this experiment?

Dependent variable ....

Independent variable ....

b Use your own results or the data provided to plot a graph of E_{cell} against $\log_{10}[Cu^{2+}]$ using the labelled grid provided (Figure 12.3).

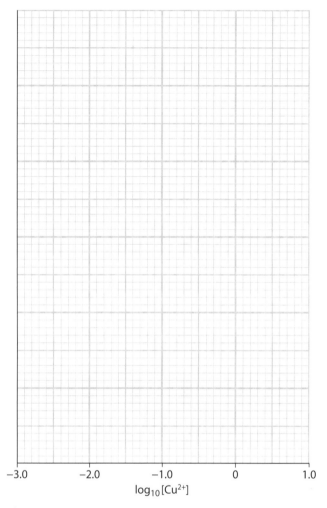

Figure 12.3

c Comment on the relationship between E_{cell} and $\log_{10}[Cu^{2+}]$

....

HINT

You will have to calculate $\log_{10}[Cu^{2+}]$ first

d Use your graph to suggest a value for E_{cell} when [ion] is 0.05 mol dm⁻³. Show on the grid above how you arrived at your answer.

....

Evaluation

e Should you use a burette or a 50 cm³ measuring cylinder when diluting the copper(II) sulfate solution? Give a reason for your answer.

....

....

f A 0.001 mol dm⁻³ solution of copper(II) sulfate can be made by diluting a 1.0 mol dm⁻³ solution tenfold using a graduated pipette then diluting this solution tenfold again to make a 0.01 mol dm⁻³ solution and then once more to make the 0.001 mol dm⁻³ solution. Comment on the accuracy of this method.

....

....

....

g Suggest an alternative method to make a very dilute solution of copper(II) sulfate which does not involve the serial dilution method described in part **f**.

....

....

....

....

Practical investigation 12.5: Planning and Data analysis
Electrical conductivity of ethanoic acid

Extension investigation

Introduction

The electrical conductivity of a solution containing ions can be measured using an electrical circuit connected to a conductivity cell (see Figure 12.4). The conductivity cell is connected to a meter which measures the conductivity of the solution directly. The conductivity of a solution depends on the area of the electrodes and the distance between the electrodes.

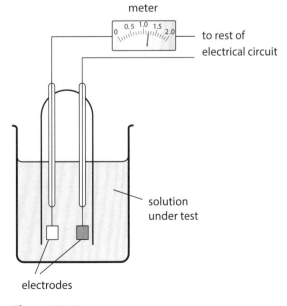

Figure 12.4

You are going to:

1 Plan an experiment to compare the electrical conductivity of solutions of ethanoic acid and sodium ethanoate

2 Analyse data about the electrical conductivity of ethanoic acid.

Method

Describe how you would carry out an experiment to compare the electrical conductivity of ethanoic acid and sodium ethanoate, stating which variables should be controlled.

You should take into account that:

• Even extremely pure water may give a small conductivity meter reading

• Movement of the solution may affect the conductivity meter reading

• Pure ethanoic acid is corrosive and flammable but ethanoic acid at concentrations below 1.7 mol dm⁻³ is low hazard. Sodium ethanoate is low hazard.

....

....

....

....

....

....

....

....

....

....

Results

Table 12.2 shows how the relative molar conductivity of ethanoic acid changes with dilution.

• Molar conductivity, Λ = conductivity $(\Omega^{-1}\,m^{-1}) \times V\,(dm^3\,mol^{-1}) \times 10^{-3}\,(dm^{-3}\,m^3)$

• Dilution, V, is the volume, in dm^3, which contains one mole of solute.

Λ / units	0.11	0.22	0.32	0.40	0.48	0.50	0.54	0.57	0.59
V / dm³ mol⁻¹	50	200	400	600	800	1000	1200	1400	1600

Table 12.2

Data analysis

a Deduce the units of molar conductivity.

> **HINT**
> Use the units in brackets in the equation for molar conductivity to work out the units

b Plot a graph of these results on the grid provided.

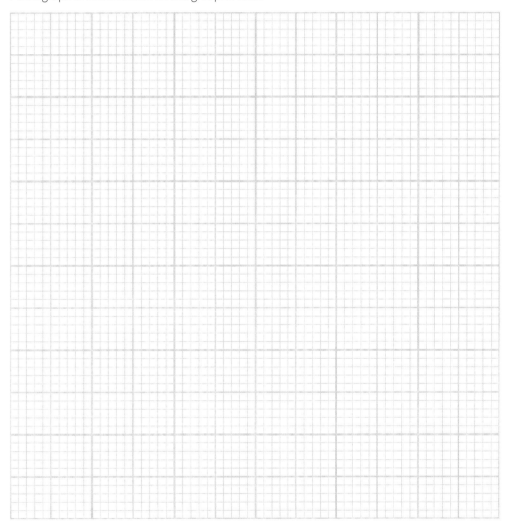

c Put a circle around any anomalous point on the graph. Explain why this point is said to be anomalous and state how you dealt with this point.

....

....

d Ethanoic acid is a weak acid. Explain the shape of the graph in terms of the extent of ionisation of ethanoic acid at different dilutions.

....

....

....

e Conductivity can be expressed by the relationship:

$$\gamma = \frac{A}{\rho l}$$

where γ is the conductivity, A is the area of the electrodes in m^2, l is the distance between the electrodes in m, and ρ is a proportionality constant.

Use this equation to suggest how conductivity depends on both the area of the electrodes and the distance between the electrodes.

....

....

....

Evaluation

f Suggest and explain one other factor which could influence the electrical conductivity of an ionic solution.

....

....

g Extremely pure water has to be used to prepare solutions whose electrical conductivity is to be measured. Suggest why extremely pure water has to be used and not tap water or distilled water.

....

h The electrodes and apparatus used in conductance experiments must be very clean. Explain why.

....

i Suggest a suitable container for storing conductivity water. Give a reason for your answer.

....

Chapter outline

This chapter relates to Chapter 21: Further aspects of equilibria and Chapter 23: Entropy and Gibbs free energy in the coursebook.

In this chapter you will complete investigations on:

- 13.1 Change in pH during an acid–base titration
- 13.2 Partition of ammonia between water and trichloromethane
- 13.3 An esterification reaction at equilibrium
- 13.4 The effect of temperature on the $N_2O_4 \rightleftharpoons 2NO_2$ equilibrium
- 13.5 Equilibrium, entropy and enthalpy change

Practical investigation 13.1:
Change in pH during an acid–base titration

Introduction

Aqueous ethanoic acid dissociates to form ethanoate ions and hydrogen ions.

$$CH_3COOH(aq) \rightleftharpoons CH_3COO^-(aq) + H^+(aq)$$

The concentration of aqueous ethanoic acid can be determined from the results of an experiment showing how pH changes when aqueous sodium hydroxide is added to the acid.

Equipment

You will need:

• 25 cm³ volumetric pipette • pipette filler • 50 cm³ burette • 100 cm³ beaker • glass stirring rod or magnetic stirrer • pH meter and pH electrode • two clamps and clamp stand for burette and pH electrode • funnel to fill burette

Access to:

• dilute ethanoic acid of unknown concentration • 0.10 mol dm⁻³ sodium hydroxide

---

Safety considerations

- Make sure you have read the advice in the Safety section at the beginning of this book and listen to any advice from your teacher before carrying out this investigation.

- Wear eye protection throughout.

- The aqueous ethanoic acid used in this experiment is low hazard.

- Sodium hydroxide at a concentration of $0.10\,mol\,dm^{-3}$ is an irritant.

Method

1   Use a pipette with a pipette filler to put $25.0\,cm^3$ of the aqueous ethanoic acid into a $100\,cm^3$ beaker.

2   Fill the burette with $0.10\,mol\,dm^{-3}$ sodium hydroxide. Record the burette reading (Table 13.1).

3   Set up the apparatus as shown in Figure 13.1. Connect the pH electrode to the pH meter and clamp it gently so that the bottom of the pH electrode is close to the base of the beaker.

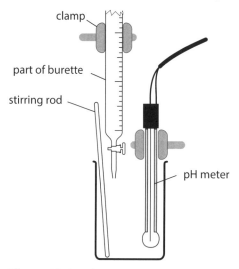

Figure 13.1

4   Record the pH.

5   Run about $2.0\,cm^3$ of sodium hydroxide from the burette into the beaker.

6   Stir the solution in the beaker with a glass rod, taking care not to hit the pH electrode. Do not remove the glass rod from the beaker.

7   Record the pH.

8   Run another $2.0\,cm^3$ of sodium hydroxide into the beaker.

9   Repeat Steps 6 and 7.

10 Continue adding the sodium hydroxide in $2.0\,cm^3$ portions with stirring and recording the pH until $34\,cm^3$ sodium hydroxide have been added.

HINT
When the pH starts increasing rapidly, add the sodium hydroxide in $0.05\,cm^3$ samples until the pH increases at a slower rate.

Results

Draw a suitable table to record your results (Table 13.1).

Table 13.1

Data analysis

a   Use the graph paper provided to plot pH against volume of sodium hydroxide added.

b   Comment on the shape of the curve and suggest which part of the curve shows the end-point of the titration.

....

....

....

....

....

c Deduce the end-point of the titration and give a reason why you chose this value.

....

....

d Use the information from the graph to describe why the end-point of this titration is not a neutral solution.

....

....

e Calculate the concentration of the aqueous ethanoic acid

Evaluation

f Put a circle around any anomalous points on your graph. State why these points are anomalous, suggest a reason and describe how you would deal with these points.

....

....

....

g Suggest an improvement in the experimental procedure which would help you determine the end-point of the titration more accurately.

....

....

....

h Why should the pH meter and glass rod be left in the beaker during the titration? To what extent would this affect the overall result?

....

....

....

i   Suggest any other improvements which could be made to this experiment in terms of either
    apparatus or how the experiment is carried out.

    ....

    ....

    ....

Practical investigation 13.2: Data analysis
Partition of ammonia between water and trichloromethane

Introduction

Water and trichloromethane, $CHCl_3$, do not mix. Ammonia is very soluble in water and slightly soluble
in trichloromethane. When an aqueous solution of ammonia is shaken with an equal volume of
trichloromethane in a separating funnel, equilibrium is eventually reached (see Figure 13.2).

$$NH_3(aq) \rightleftharpoons NH_3(CHCl_3)$$

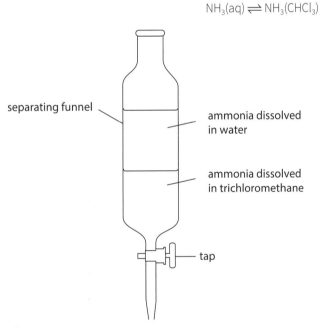

separating funnel

ammonia dissolved
in water

ammonia dissolved
in trichloromethane

tap

Figure 13.2

The equilibrium expression for this process is called the partition coefficient.

The concentration of ammonia in each layer can be found by removing a fixed volume of the
solution from each layer and titrating the ammonia with a standard solution of hydrochloric acid.
If the volume of each solution removed is replaced with an equal volume of each solvent, the
experiment can be repeated. The experiment was repeated like this seven times.

Safety considerations

1 Trichloromethane is harmful. Its boiling point is 62 °C.

2 Ammonia is low hazard at concentrations less than 3.0 mol dm^{-3}. Its boiling point is −33 °C.

You are going to analyse the data provided, interpret the results and evaluate the experiment.

Safety

What precautions would you take to make sure that the experiment is performed safely?

....

....

....

Results

Experiment number	Concentration of ammonia in aqueous layer / mol dm^{-3}	Concentration of ammonia in trichloromethane layer / mol dm^{-3}
1	1.85	0.080
2	1.49	0.065
3	1.09	0.047
4	0.92	0.040
5	0.68	0.030
6	0.51	0.022
7	0.40	0.017
8	0.35	0.012
9	0.24	0.005

Table 13.2

Data analysis

You are going to plot a graph of the concentration of ammonia in the aqueous layer against the concentration of ammonia in the trichloromethane layer.

a First predict the shape of the graph. Explain your answer.

....

....

HINT

Plot the concentration of ammonia in the aqueous layer on the vertical axis. Don't forget to label your axes

b Using the graph paper provided, plot a graph to show how the concentration of ammonia in the aqueous layer changes as the concentration of ammonia in the trichloromethane layer increases.

c Use your graph to calculate a value for the partition coefficient

$$\frac{[NH_3(aq)]}{[NH_3(CHCl_3)]}$$

d On the grid provided, extrapolate the line to reach the 0,0 point. Calculate the percentage deviation of the experimental line from the extrapolated line when the concentration of the ammonia in trichloromethane is 0.01 mol dm^{-3} by using the relationship:

$$\frac{\text{Experimental value - Extrapolated value} \times 100}{\text{Extrapolated value}}$$

Evaluation

e What essential piece of glassware is missing from the diagram at the start of this investigation? Explain why this is essential.

....

....

f The deviations from the extrapolated line at low concentrations may not be anomalous results. Use the information from your graph to explain why they are unlikely to be anomalous.

....

....

g How could you make sure that the deviation in the line at very low concentrations was not due to experimental error?

....

....

h The whole experiment was not repeated. Suggest:

- Why the results are valid without repeating the experiment.

....

....

- Why the results may not be valid unless the whole experiment is repeated.

....

i Name one variable that has not been controlled in this experiment and give a reason why it should be controlled.

....

....

....

Practical investigation 13.3: Planning
An esterification reaction at equilibrium

Introduction

When ethyl ethanoate reacts with water, an equilibrium is formed.

$$CH_3COOC_2H_5 + H_2O \rightleftharpoons CH_3COOH + C_2H_5OH$$
ethyl ethanoate   ethanoic acid   ethanol

The reaction can be speeded up by the addition of a catalyst of hydrochloric acid.

At the start of the reaction only ethyl ethanoate and water are present. As the reaction proceeds, the concentration of ethanoic acid and ethanol increases and concentration of ethyl ethanoate and water decreases until equilibrium is reached. This takes about one week.

You are going to:

- Plan a series of experiments to determine the number of moles of each of these reactants and products at equilibrium.

- Analyse data about the number of moles of each of these substances at equilibrium in order to determine the equilibrium constant.

Method

Answer the following questions about how you would carry out a series of experiments to determine the number of moles of each of these reactants and products at equilibrium using different initial amounts of ethyl ethanoate and water.

Use the following information to help you:

- You are given pure ethyl ethanoate, $6.0 \, mol \, dm^{-3}$ hydrochloric acid (corrosive) and distilled water.

- The same experiment should be repeated using different initial amounts of ethyl ethanoate and water.

- Pure ethanoic acid is corrosive, volatile and flammable but ethanoic acid at concentrations between 1.7 and $4.0 \, mol \, dm^{-3}$ is an irritant; below $1.7 \, mol \, dm^{-3}$ it is low hazard. Ethyl ethanoate is volatile, flammable and dissolves plastics and rubber. Pure ethanol is volatile and highly flammable but a dilute solution is low hazard.

- The amount of acid at the beginning and end of the experiment can be found by titration.

1 Suggest the quantities of each substance to be used at the start of each experiment.

....

....

....

2 What safety precautions do you need to take?

....

....

....

3 Describe how you will carry out the experiment and determine the concentration of ethanoic acid at equilibrium?

....

....

....

....

....

157

....

....

....

....

....

Results

Table 13.3 gives the results of a series of similar experiments starting with only ethanol and ethanoic acid. The experiments were carried out at temperatures between 110 °C and 130 °C in sealed glass tubes.

$$CH_3COOH + C_2H_5OH \rightleftharpoons CH_3COOC_2H_5 + H_2O$$

Moles of CH_3COOH at start	Moles of C_2H_5OH at start	Moles of $CH_3COOC_2H_5$ at equilibrium	Moles of CH_3COOH at equilibrium	Moles of C_2H_5OH at equilibrium	K_a
1.00	0.18	0.17			
1.00	0.50	0.42			
1.00	0.33	0.29			
1.00	2.00	0.84			
1.00	8.00	0.96			

Table 13.3

Data analysis

> **HINT**
>
> For every one mole of $CH_3COOC_2H_5$ formed, one mole of CH_3COOH and one mole of C_2H_5OH are removed from the mixture at the start

a Complete Table 13.3 by deducing the number of moles of CH_3COOH and C_2H_5OH at equilibrium (columns 4 and 5).

b The number of moles of water at equilibrium is the same as the number of moles of ethyl ethanoate. Explain why.

....

c Write the equilibrium expression in terms of concentration for this reaction.

d Explain why the number of moles can be used instead of concentration in this expression.

e Complete Table 13.3 by calculating the values of K_a in the last column.

Evaluation

f Explain why the experiments were carried out in sealed tubes.

....

....

g In this experiment, the volume was kept constant. Suggest one other variable in this experiment that should be controlled and suggest how it could be controlled.

....

....

h The number of moles of acid in the tubes at equilibrium can be found by titration. What must you do to the tubes before you carry out the titration?

....

....

i Compare the values of K_a obtained in this experiment. To what extent does the data support the idea that K_a is constant when different numbers of moles of ethanoic acid and ethanol are left to reach equilibrium. Give reasons to back up your answer.

....

....

....

j Suggest why the reaction was carried out at over 100 °C and not at room temperature.

....

....

Practical investigation 13.4: Planning
The effect of temperature on the $N_2O_4 \rightleftharpoons 2NO_2$ equilibrium

Introduction

Nitrogen dioxide, NO_2, and dinitrogen tetroxide, N_2O_4, form an equilibrium mixture at room temperature.

$$N_2O_4 \rightleftharpoons 2NO_2 \ \Delta H = +58 \text{ kJ mol}^{-1}$$

You are going to:

- Plan an experiment to prepare a sample of liquid N_2O_4

- Then use this to fill a gas syringe with nitrogen dioxide

- Suggest how you could use the syringe with nitrogen dioxide in it to demonstrate the effect of temperature on the $N_2O_4 \rightleftharpoons 2NO_2$ equilibrium

The following information will be useful in answering the questions that follow:

- Nitrogen dioxide can be produced by heating lead nitrate, $Pb(NO_3)_2$

- $2Pb(NO_3)_2(s) \rightarrow 2PbO(s) + 4NO_2(g) + O_2(g)$

- Dinitrogen tetroxide, N_2O_4, is a light yellow toxic liquid which boils at 21 °C.

- Nitrogen dioxide, NO_2, is a brown toxic gas at room temperature. It decomposes above 150 °C. It is very soluble in water.

- Lead nitrate is toxic.

Equipment

- You are provided with lead nitrate and have access to common laboratory apparatus.

- The equipment needs to be capable of collecting the N_2O_4 and NO_2 safely.

- You will need three taps to control the flow of the nitrogen dioxide through the apparatus.

You need not list the equipment here but it must be labelled when drawing it in the Method section.

Safety considerations

- What precautions would you take to make sure that the experiment is performed safely?

....

....

....

Method

1 Draw a labelled diagram to show the arrangement of the apparatus used to collect the N_2O_4.

2 Describe how you would carry out the experiment.

....

....

....

....

....

3 Draw a labelled diagram to show the arrangement of the apparatus used to convert the N_2O_4 to NO_2 and collect the NO_2 in a gas syringe.

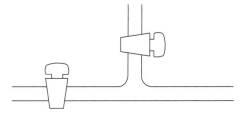

Figure 13.3

4 Describe how you would carry out the experiment.

....

....

....

5 Describe how you could use the syringe with nitrogen dioxide in the experiment to demonstrate the effect of temperature on the $N_2O_4 \rightleftharpoons 2NO_2$ equilibrium. Include a prediction of what you might observe.

....

....

....

....

....

....

....

Data analysis

a State an appropriate volume of nitrogen dioxide that should be collected in the syringe.

....

b Calculate the number of moles of nitrogen dioxide present in the volume you chose in part **a**.

> **HINT**
> One mole of any gas occupies 24.0 dm³ at room temperature and pressure

= .... mol

c Calculate the minimum mass of lead nitrate that needs to be heated to produce the number of moles of nitrogen dioxide you calculated in part **b**.

> **HINT**
> You need to refer to the equation at the start of the investigation. A_r values: N = 14.0, O = 16.0, Pb = 207.2

= .... g

Evaluation

d The liquid N_2O_4 is collected in a tube. Oxygen will also be present in this tube and air may also be present. Explain why.

....

....

e When converting liquid N_2O_4 to NO_2, some of the NO_2 gas may escape into the air. Suggest a method of absorbing this NO_2 gas.

....

....

f Why is it important that air is removed from the connecting tubes and gas syringe?

....

....

g Why should the apparatus and lead nitrate be completely dry?

....

....

h Comment on whether this investigation into how temperature affects the $N_2O_4 \rightleftharpoons 2NO_2$ equilibrium is likely to be effective or not. Suggest any difficulties in interpreting the results.

....

....

....

Practical investigation 13.5: Data analysis
Equilibrium, entropy and enthalpy change

Introduction

The relationship between the equilibrium constant, entropy and enthalpy change can be expressed by the relationship:

$$\ln K_p = -\frac{\Delta H^\ominus}{RT} + \frac{\Delta S^\ominus}{T}$$

HINT

$\ln = 2.303 \times \log_{10}$

Where $\ln K_p$ is the natural logarithm of the equilibrium constant;

$\Delta H^\ominus$ is the standard enthalpy change of reaction; $\Delta S^\ominus$ is the standard entropy change of the reaction;

R is the molar gas constant; T is the temperature in kelvin

This relationship can be used to study the variation of the equilibrium constant with temperature for the reaction:

$$N_2(g) + O_2(g) \rightleftharpoons 2NO(g)$$

You are going to complete a table of data and analyse this graphically to draw conclusions.

Results

Table 13.4 shows some values of K_p for the above reaction at different temperatures.

Temperature /K	$\dfrac{1}{\text{Temperature}}$ / K^{-1}	K_p	$\ln K_p$
1800		1.21×10^{-4}	
2000		4.08×10^{-4}	
2200		11.00×10^{-4}	
2400		30.10×10^{-4}	
2600		50.30×10^{-4}	
2800		81.52×10^{-4}	

Table 13.4

163

Data analysis

a Complete Table 13.4 to show the reciprocal of the temperature and ln K_p

b Plot a graph to show how ln K_p varies with $\frac{1}{T}$.

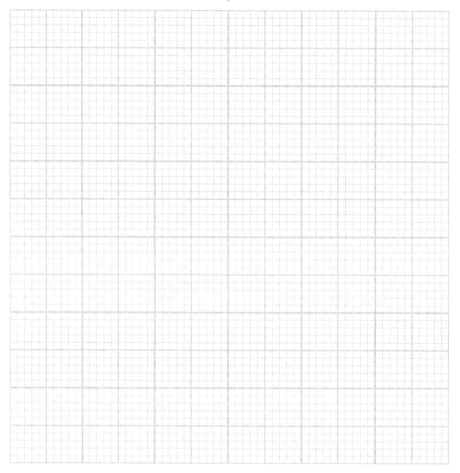

HINT

Plot ln K_p on the vertical axis. Don't forget to label your axes!

c Determine a value for the gradient of the graph. Show on your graph how you arrived at your answer.

d The gradient of the graph is $-\dfrac{\Delta H^\ominus}{R}$

Calculate the value of $\Delta H^\ominus$ in kJ mol^{-1} for the reaction.

HINT

$R = 8.314\ \text{J K}^{-1}\,\text{mol}^{-1}$

Evaluation

e Does the graph you have plotted show any anomalous points? Explain your answer.

....

....

f When the graph line, from the data given, is extrapolated to reach the y-axis when $\frac{1}{T}$ is zero, the value of the entropy change for the reaction can be calculated. Suggest why significant errors may arise from this extrapolation and what you could do to reduce this error.

....

....

Chapter 14:
Reaction kinetics

Chapter outline

This chapter relates to Chapter 22: Reaction kinetics in the coursebook.

In this chapter you will complete investigations on:

- 14.1 Kinetics of the reaction between propanone and iodine
- 14.2 Rate of decomposition of an organic compound
- 14.3 Determination of the order of a reaction
- 14.4 Effect of temperature on rate of reaction

Practical investigation 14.1:
Kinetics of the reaction between propanone and iodine

Introduction

In the presence of acid, propanone reacts with iodine.

$$CH_3COCH_3(aq) + I_2(aq) \rightarrow CH_3COCH_2I(aq) + HI(aq)$$

The kinetics of this reaction can be analysed by measuring the initial rate of change of concentration of iodine. The rate of change is proportional to the volume of iodine used in the reaction and inversely proportional to the time taken for the colour of the iodine to disappear.

Equipment

You will need:

• 100 cm³ conical flask, • stopclock or stopwatch • test tube or boiling tube • two 10 cm³ measuring cylinders • 20 cm³ or 50 cm³ measuring cylinder • white tile or piece of white paper • three sticky labels

Access to:

• 2.0 mol dm⁻³ propanone • 2.0 mol dm⁻³ hydrochloric acid • 0.01 mol dm⁻³ aqueous iodine • distilled water • burette for dispensing distilled water

---

Safety considerations

- Make sure you have read the advice in the Safety section at the beginning of this book and listen to any advice from your teacher before carrying out this investigation.

- Propanone is highly flammable and irritant.

- Dilute iodine solution is low hazard.

Method

You will do four similar experiments using different volumes of the reaction mixture as shown in Table 14.1.

	Experiment A	Experiment B	Experiment C	Experiment D
Volume of 2.0 mol dm^{-3} propanone / cm^3	10	5	10	10
Volume of 2.0 mol dm^{-3} hydrochloric acid / cm^3	20	20	10	20
Volume of water / cm^3	2.5	5	10	0

Table 14.1

1   Label one small measuring cylinder for use with propanone, one small measuring cylinder for use with iodine and the larger measuring cylinder for the hydrochloric acid.

2   Set up flask A with 10.0 cm^3 propanone, 20 cm^3 hydrochloric acid and 2.5 cm^3 water. Place the flask on a white tile or piece of white paper.

3   Measure out 2.5 cm^3 of 0.01 mol dm^{-3} aqueous iodine into a test tube.

4   Pour the aqueous iodine into the flask and immediately start the stopclock and swirl the flask.

5   Time how long it takes until you can no longer see the colour of the iodine. Record this in Table 14.2.

6   Wash out the flask with distilled water and dry it.

7   Repeat the procedure for Experiments B, C and D using the volumes shown in the table above but use 5 cm^3 of 0.01 mol dm^{-3} aqueous iodine. Record your results in Table 14.2.

Results

	Experiment A	Experiment B	Experiment C	Experiment D
Time for colour of iodine to disappear /s				
Relative rate of reaction in cm^3 I$_2$ /s				

Table 14.2

Data analysis

a   When calculating the relative rate of reaction why does the volume of iodine have to be taken into account?

....

....

b   Suggest why this experiment is valid whatever the order of reaction?

....

....

HINT

The second row can be calculated using the information in the introduction c Use your results, together with the information in Table 14.2, to determine the order of reaction with respect to propanone, iodine and hydrochloric acid and the overall order of reaction. Explain your answers.

....

....

....

....

....

....

....

....

d Write the overall rate equation for this reaction.

....

e Suggest why hydrochloric acid appears in the overall rate equation but not in the equation in the introduction section.

....

Evaluation

f Water does not appear in the rate equation. Suggest why different volumes of water were added in the experiment.

....

g Refer to the equipment used to suggest how the accuracy of the experiment could be improved?

....

....

....

h Apart from errors in measurements, suggest two other sources of error in this experiment and how these errors can be minimised.

....

....

....

Practical investigation 14.2: Data analysis
Rate of decomposition of an organic compound

Extension investigation

Introduction

In the presence of a sodium hydroxide catalyst, compound **Z** (4-hydroxy-4-methylpentan-2-one) decomposes to propanone. As the reaction proceeds, there is a small change in the volume of the reaction mixture. This can be measured using a dilatometer (see Figure 14.1).

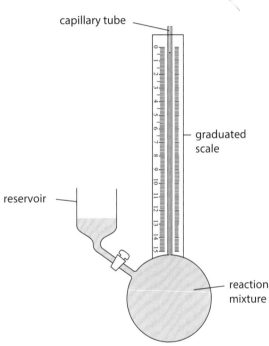

Figure 14.1

- Excess compound Z was added to 0.20 mol dm⁻³ aqueous sodium hydroxide.

- The reaction mixture was placed in a glass bulb connected to a capillary tube. The reaction mixture reached slightly above the bottom of the capillary tube.

- The tap was closed and the dilatometer was placed in a thermostatically controlled water bath.

- When the temperature was constant, readings were taken at particular time intervals.

- The experiment was repeated using aqueous sodium hydroxide of concentration 0.05 mol dm⁻³. All other conditions remained the same.

- The difference between the final dilatometer, r_f reading and the dilatometer reading at time t (r_t), is related to the rate constant by the formula:

$$\log_{10}(r_f - r_t) = -\frac{kt}{2.303} + c$$

- Where k is the rate constant, t is the time and c is a constant.

169

Data analysis

Table 14.3 shows how the dilatometer readings in millimetres change with time in minutes.

Reaction using 0.20 mol dm⁻³ sodium hydroxide				Reaction using 0.05 mol dm⁻³ sodium hydroxide			
Time / min	Dilatometer reading / cm	$r_f - r_t$ / cm	$\log_{10}(r_f - r_t)$	Time / min	Dilatometer reading / cm	$r_f - r_t$ / cm	$\log_{10}(r_f - r_t)$
0	0.2			0	0.3		
2	0.9			5	0.8		
4	1.5			10	1.8		
6	2.0			15	2.7		
8	2.4			20	2.8		
10	2.7			25	3.5		
12	3.0			30	3.7		
14	3.2			35	4.2		
16	3.4			40	4.3		
18	3.6			45	4.4		
38	4.2			85	6.3		
40	4.2			90	6.3		

Table 14.3

a Complete the third and seventh columns in Table 14.3 to calculate the values of $r_f - r_t$ for each concentration of sodium hydroxide.

b Complete the fourth and eighth columns in Table 14.3 to calculate the values of $\log_{10}(r_f - r_t)$ for each concentration of sodium hydroxide.

c   Using Figure 14.2, plot a graph of $\log_{10}(r_f - r_t)$ against time for the reaction using 0.20 mol dm^{-3} sodium hydroxide.

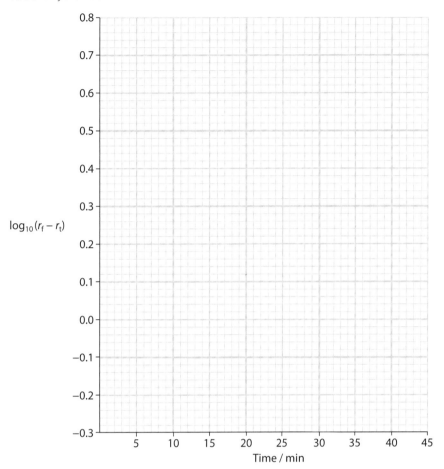

Figure 14.2

d   On the same axes, plot the points for $\log_{10}(r_f - r_t)$ against time for the reaction using 0.05 mol dm^{-3} sodium hydroxide.

e   The reaction using 0.2 mol dm^{-3} sodium hydroxide is first order with respect to sodium hydroxide.

Suggest why plotting $\log_{10}(r_f - r_t)$ against time is a better method than plotting $(r_f - r_t)$ against time.

....

....

....

f   Explain why this is not the overall order of reaction.

....

....

Evaluation

g Comment on the variability of the data for the reaction using $0.05\,mol\,dm^{-3}$ sodium hydroxide and whether it is sufficient to show that the reaction is first order. Explain your answer by referring to the points on the graph.

....

....

....

h Explain why the control of temperature is particularly important in this method.

....

....

i Suggest any other problems specific to this method which may lead to inaccurate or variable results.

....

....

Practical investigation 14.3: Planning
Determination of the order of a reaction

Introduction

Calcium carbonate reacts with hydrochloric acid:

$$CaCO_3(s) + 2HCl(aq) \rightarrow CaCl_2(aq) + CO_2(g) + H_2O(l)$$

You are going to plan and carry out an experiment to determine the order of this reaction with respect to hydrochloric acid. Use sources of information such as textbooks or the internet to plan this experiment. You are provided with calcium carbonate as marble chips (pieces of marble) and hydrochloric acid of concentration $2.0\,mol\,dm^{-3}$.

Equipment

What equipment will you need?

• Draw a diagram in the space provided of the apparatus that you will use.

• Label the pieces of apparatus in your diagram.

• Make a list of the equipment you will need.

- Suggest an appropriate mass and size of calcium carbonate to use and suitable volumes and concentrations of hydrochloric acid.

Equipment

- ....

- ....

- ....

- ....

- ....

- ....

- ....

- ....

- ....

- ....

Mass, volumes and concentration of reagents used: give reasons why you chose these quantities.

....

....

....

....

Safety considerations

How will you carry out the experiment safely?

....

....

Method

Give details of how you will carry out the experiment.

....

....

....

....

....

....

Identify the:

• Independent variable

....

• Dependent variable

....

• Other variables that need to be controlled and how these should be controlled.

....

....

....

Results

Construct a table of results (Table 14.4) in the space provided which will enable you to see how the rate of this reaction changes with concentration of hydrochloric acid.

Table 14.4

HINT
Remember that rate is inversely proportional to time

Data analysis

a Use the graph paper provided to plot one or more graphs which will help you determine the order of reaction with respect to hydrochloric acid.

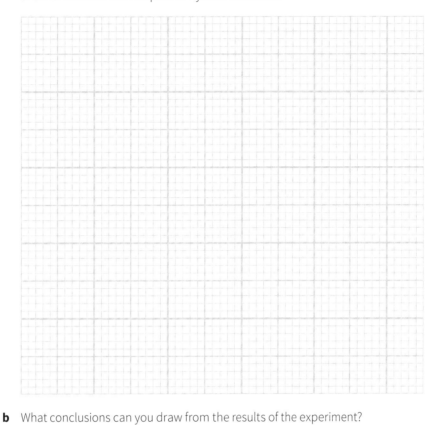

b What conclusions can you draw from the results of the experiment?

....

....

....

....

Evaluation

c Comment on the variability of your data

....

....

d What were the weaknesses of the experimental procedure that you used? Explain your answer.

....

....

....

....

Practical investigation 14.4: Planning
Effect of temperature on rate of reaction

Introduction

Sodium thiosulfate and hydrochloric acid react to produce a precipitate of sulfur.

$$Na_2S_2O_3(aq) + 2HCl(aq) \rightarrow S(s) + SO_2(g) + H_2O(l) + 2NaCl(aq)$$

Sodium thiosulfate and hydrochloric acid are colourless. Sulfur dioxide is a toxic gas.

The precipitate is seen as a cloudy suspension in the solution and takes some time to settle. As the reaction proceeds, the solution gets cloudier and cloudier.

You are going to plan and carry out a series of experiments to investigate how the rate of this reaction changes with temperature.

Equipment

What equipment will you need?

•   Draw a diagram, in the space provided, of the apparatus that you will use.

•   Label the pieces of apparatus in your diagram.

•   Make a list of the equipment you will need.

•   Suggest appropriate volumes and concentrations of each of the reagents that you use.

Labelled apparatus set-up

Equipment list

•   ....

•   ....

•   ....

•   ....

•   ....

•   ....

•   ....

•   ....

•   ....

•   ....

Reagents

....

....

Safety considerations

How will you carry out the experiment safely and how will you dispose of the reaction mixtures?

....

....

....

Method

Give details of how you will carry out the experiment.

....

....

....

....

....

....

> **HINT**
> Before you carry out any experiments, make sure that your plan has been checked by your teacher

Identify the:

- Independent variable

  ....

- Dependent variable

  ....

- Other variables that need to be controlled

  ....

  ....

Results

Predict your results using ideas about particle collisions.

....

....

....

Suggest why the procedure used will be effective.

....

....

Construct a table of results (Table 14.5) in the space provided which will enable you to see how the rate of this reaction changes with temperature.

Table 14.5

Data analysis

a Use the grid provided to plot a graph of your results.

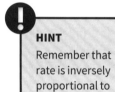

HINT
Remember that rate is inversely proportional to time

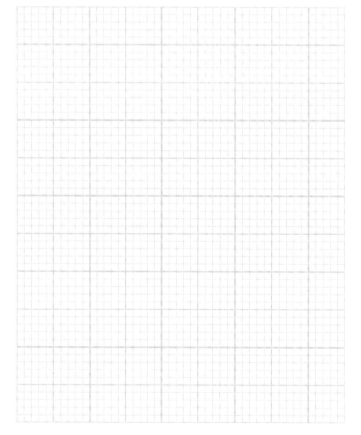

b What conclusions can you draw from the results of the experiment? Refer to your graph and other data to support your answer.

....

....

....

....

c Describe how closely the results of your experiment agreed with your predictions.

....

....

Evaluation

d What were the weaknesses of the experimental procedure that you used? Explain your answer.

....

....

....

....

e Was the data you collected sufficient to support your predictions and conclusions? Explain your answer.

....

....

....

f What improvements should you make to your experimental method?

....

....

....

....

Transition elements

Chapter outline

This chapter relates to Chapter 24: Transition elements in the coursebook.

In this chapter you will complete investigations on:

- 15.1 Copper content of copper ore
- 15.2 Analysis of iron tablets
- 15.3 Formula of a complex ion
- 15.4 Reaction of copper with potassium dichromate(VI)

Practical investigation 15.1: Planning
Copper content of copper ore

Introduction

Malachite is an ore of copper. It is mainly basic copper carbonate $CuCO_3Cu(OH)_2$. The ore also contains materials such as silicon dioxide, which do not react with acids.

You are going to plan an experiment to:

- produce an aqueous solution of copper(II) sulfate from a 20 g sample of malachite

- determine the approximate mass of copper ions present in this 20 g sample by comparing the colour of your copper sulfate solution with solutions of copper(II) sulfate of known concentration.

Equipment

You are provided with solutions of $2.0\,mol\,dm^{-3}$ sulfuric acid and $1.0\,mol\,dm^{-3}$ aqueous copper(II) sulfate and distilled water. You also have access to common laboratory equipment.

List the equipment and any additional substances required to produce an aqueous solution of copper(II) sulfate from a 20 g sample of malachite.

- ....
- ....
- ....
- ....

- ....
- ....
- ....
- ....

Method

1   Describe how you would carry out this experiment. Include any safety considerations giving reasons.

....

....

....

....

....

....

....

2   Describe the method you would use to determine the approximate concentration of your solution of aqueous copper(II) sulfate. You do **not** have access to a colorimeter.

....

....

....

....

....

....

....

....

> **HINT**
> This is about moles, volumes and concentrations

Data analysis

a Describe how you will process your results to obtain a value for the approximate mass of copper ions present in this 20 g sample of malachite. (A_r Cu = 63.5)

....

....

....

....

....

Evaluation

b Should you use a 20 cm³ measuring cylinder or a burette when diluting the copper(II) sulfate solution? Give a reason for your answer.

....

....

c Apart from using glassware of appropriate accuracy or using a colorimeter, suggest how you could determine the concentration of your solution more accurately.

....

....

....

d How can you be sure that you are comparing your solutions in a fair way? Explain your answer.

....

....

e Explain the weakness of this experimental procedure.

....

....

....

Practical investigation 15.2: Data analysis
Analysis of iron tablets

Introduction

People who do not have enough iron in their blood can take iron tablets. Iron tablets contain Fe^{2+} ions, insoluble materials and substances which help bind the particles together.

We can calculate the percentage of Fe^{2+} ions in iron tablets by reacting an acidified solution obtained from the tablets with manganate(VII) ions:

$$MnO_4^-(aq) + 8H^+(aq) + 5Fe^{2+}(aq) \rightarrow Mn^{2+}(aq) + 5Fe^{3+}(aq) + 4H_2O(l)$$

A solution of potassium manganate(VII) is purple. Aqueous Mn^{2+} ions are almost colourless, aqueous Fe^{2+} ions are very pale green and aqueous Fe^{3+} ions are very pale yellow.

Method

1 Record the mass of an iron tablet to the nearest 0.01 g.

2 Grind the tablet in a mortar with few cm^3 of 1.0 mol dm^{-3} sulfuric acid to obtain a paste.

3 Transfer the paste to a 100 cm^3 volumetric flask and make the volume up to 100 cm^3 by adding more 1.0 mol dm^{-3} sulfuric acid.

4 Take a 10.0 cm^3 portion of the solution and titrate with 0.0050 mol dm^{-3} aqueous potassium manganate(VII). The end-point of the titration is when a permanent purple colour is first seen.

5 Repeat the titration with further 10.0 cm^3 portions of the solution.

Data analysis

The titration results are shown in Table 15.1 using a tablet of mass 0.58 g.

	Run 1	Run 2	Run 3	Run 4
Initial burette reading / cm^3	0.10	5.15	9.65	14.85
Final burette reading / cm^3	5.25	9.65	14.85	19.70
Titre / cm^3				

Table 15.1

a Complete Table 15.1.

b Explain why an indicator is not needed in this titration.

....

....

c Run 1 is the rough titration. Suggest why this should be ignored when calculating the average titre.

....

....

d Comment on the variability of the results and suggest what should be done to reduce this variability.

....

....

....

e Use the data for Run 2 to calculate the moles of MnO_4^- (aq) ion and from this the number of moles of Fe^{2+}(aq) ions in 10 cm^3 of solution.

f Deduce the number of moles of Fe^{2+} ions present in the volumetric flask.

g Calculate the percentage by mass of Fe^{2+} ions present in the iron tablet. A_r Fe = 55.8

Evaluation

h Suggest why the iron tablet was made up in sulfuric acid rather than water.

....

....

i Suggest how all the iron tablet paste can be transferred to the volumetric flask to minimise the loss of Fe^{2+}(aq) ions.

....

....

....

j How would you make sure that the contents of the volumetric flask are completely mixed?

....

....

k Explain how you would obtain a 10.0 cm^3 portion of the solution for titration.

....

....

l   A brown colour may develop if not enough acid is present. Why is it important that this brown colour is removed?

....

....

m   Describe and explain any other sources of error in this experiment.

....

....

....

....

Practical investigation 15.3: Data analysis
Formula of a complex ion

Introduction

The concentration of a coloured solution can be determined by colorimetry. A colorimeter (see Figure 15.1) measures the transmittance of light through a cell containing the coloured substance. The less concentrated the coloured solution, the more light is transmitted through the cell.

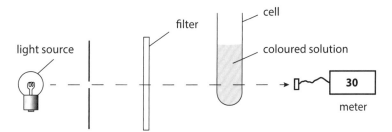

Figure 15.1

The relationship between the concentration of a coloured substance in solution and the intensity of light transmitted through the cell is:

$$log_{10}\frac{I_o}{I} = kC$$

where I_o is the light transmitted through the pure solvent, I is the light transmitted through the solution, k is a proportionality constant and C is the concentration of the coloured substance.

We can find the ratio in which Ni^{2+} ions combine with $EDTA^{4-}$ ions (ethylenediaminetetracetate ions) to form a complex ion by a continuous variation method.

*   Aqueous solutions containing different volumes of $0.05\ mol\ dm^{-3}$ Ni^{2+} ions and $0.05\ mol\ dm^{-3}$ $EDTA^{4-}$ ions are made.

*   A filter is chosen which is appropriate for the colour of the complex ion formed.

*   A cell containing water is placed in the colorimeter and the colorimeter reading is set to 100% transmission.

- The cell is washed and dried and filled with a solution containing $0\,cm^3$ Ni^{2+} ions and $10\,cm^3$ $EDTA^{4-}$ ions and the colorimeter reading is recorded.

- The process is repeated using different volumes of Ni^{2+} ions and $EDTA^{4-}$ ions.

Data analysis

The results are shown in Table 15.2

Volume of 0.05 mol dm⁻³ Ni²⁺ ions / cm³	Volume of 0.05 mol dm⁻³ EDTA⁴⁻ ions / cm³	Colorimeter reading / % transmittance	$\dfrac{I_o}{I}$	$\log_{10} \dfrac{I_o}{I}$
0	10	100		
1	9	74		
2	8	55		
3	7	50		
4	6	23		
5	5	22		
6	4	26		
7	3	35		
8	2	39		
9	1	63		
10	0	91		

Table 15.2

a Complete the third and fourth columns in the table.

b Using Figure 15.2, plot a graph of $\log_{10} \dfrac{I_o}{I}$ against the mole proportion of Ni^{2+} and $EDTA^{4-}$ in the solution.

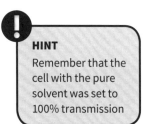

HINT
Remember that the cell with the pure solvent was set to 100% transmission

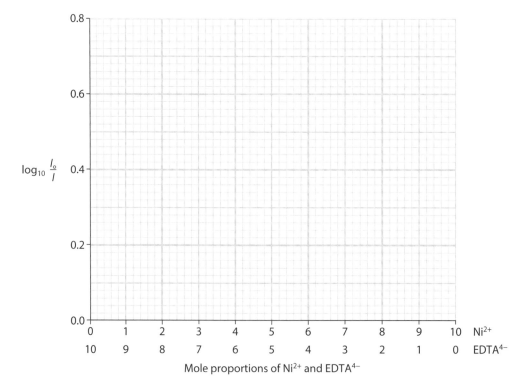

Figure 15.2

c At which mole proportion of Ni^{2+} to $EDTA^{4-}$ was the colorimeter reading greatest?

Suggest why.

....

....

Evaluation

d A student suggested that the meter reading may not be proportional to the concentration of the solution. Suggest how you could test this hypothesis.

....

....

e Suggest why it is not necessary to know the absolute concentration of the complex formed.

....

....

....

f A student suggested that the complex of nickel and $EDTA^{4-}$ contains equimolar amounts of nickel and $EDTA^{4-}$. Give points for and against this argument.

....

....

....

....

g How could you improve the experiment to be certain that the correct molar ratio of nickel to $EDTA^{4-}$ had been determined?

....

....

h Suggest why the meter reading was set to 100% transmittance using water alone.

....

i In some old colorimeters, the samples could be placed in eleven test tubes instead of being placed in a cell. Suggest why the use of test tubes may give inaccurate results.

....

....

....

Practical investigation 15.4: Planning
Reaction of copper with potassium dichromate(VI)

Introduction

Copper reacts with acidified potassium dichromate, which contains dichromate(VI) ions, $Cr_2O_7^{2-}$, to form Cu^{2+} ions and Cr^{3+} ions.

$$3Cu(s) + Cr_2O_7^{2-}(aq) + 14H^+(aq) \rightarrow 3Cu^{2+}(aq) + 2Cr^{3+}(aq) + 7H_2O(l)$$

The reaction can be followed by measuring the changes in the transmittance of light at different wavelengths in the visible region of the spectrum as the orange dichromate(VI) ions change to a mixture of Cu^{2+} ions and Cr^{3+} ions. Samples of the reaction mixture are taken at regular intervals for analysis by visible absorption spectroscopy. The rate of reaction can be obtained from the results. The visible absorption spectrum of Cr^{3+} ions is shown in Figure 15.3

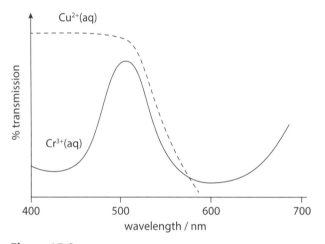

Figure 15.3

You are going to plan an experiment to:

- Follow the changes in concentration of the $Cr_2O_7^{2-}$, Cu^{2+} and Cr^{3+} ions as the reaction proceeds.

- Calculate suitable volumes and concentrations for each component of the reaction mixture so that the potassium dichromate is the limiting reagent, the potassium dichromate concentration should be less than $0.03\,mol\,dm^{-3}$.

Equipment

You are provided with copper foil, solid potassium dichromate(VI) and $2.0\,mol\,dm^{-3}$ sulfuric acid. You also have access to common laboratory equipment.

List the equipment and any additional substances required for the experiment.

- ....
- ....
- ....
- ....

- ....
- ....
- ....
- ....

Method

Suggest suitable volumes and concentrations for each component of the reaction mixture. Relative formula masses: $Cu = 63.5$, $K_2Cr_2O_7 = 294.2$, $H_2SO_4 = 98.1$.

Describe how you would carry out this experiment. Include any safety considerations.

....

....

....

....

....

....

....

....

> **HINT**
>
> $2.0\,mol\,dm^{-3}$ sulfuric acid is corrosive. Solid potassium dichromate(VI) is very toxic and oxidising and solutions of moderately low concentration are toxic. Copper is low hazard.

189

Data analysis

Figure 15.4 shows how percentage transmittance changes with wavelength using a sample taken at the start of the reaction and a sample taken when the reaction is nearly complete.

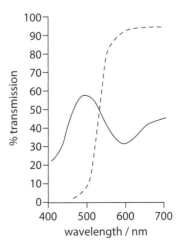

Figure 15.4

a On Figure 15.4, identify the spectrum at the start of the reaction by the letter *S* and the spectrum near the completion of the reaction by the letter *C*.

b On Figure 15.4, draw the spectrum that you would observe when the reaction is about half complete. Explain the line you drew in terms of the transmission of light of different colours through the reaction mixture.

....

....

....

c Explain how the order of reaction with respect to dichromate ions could be obtained by using this method.

....

....

....

Evaluation

d The spectrometer has two cells, one for the sample and one for water. Explain why.

....

....

e Identify two variables which should be controlled in this experiment. Explain why each should be controlled.

....

....

....

f Explain why using the sampling technique in this experiment is **not** a problem.

....

....

g Suggest, apart from reasons of safety, why the concentration of the potassium dichromate VI should be very low.

....

....

Chapter 16:
More about organic chemistry

Chapter outline

This chapter relates to Chapters 25: Benzene and its compounds, Chapter 26: Carboxylic acids and their derivatives, Chapter 27: Organic nitrogen compounds and Chapter 28: Polymerisation in the coursebook.

In this chapter you will complete investigations on:

- 16.1 Making an azo dye
- 16.2 Acylation of a nucleic acid
- 16.3 Nitration of benzene

Practical investigation 16.1: Planning
Making an azo dye

Introduction

The azo dye benzene-azo-2 naphthol can be made from 2-naphthol (a phenol) and phenylamine in a two stage process.

The first step is the reaction between phenylamine (dissolved in $2\,mol\,dm^{-3}$ hydrochloric acid) and nitrous acid to give a diazonium salt:

$$C_6H_5NH_2 + HNO_2 + HCl \rightarrow C_6H_5N^+{\equiv}NCl^- + 2H_2O$$

Nitrous acid is unstable, so it has to be made during the experiment by adding sodium nitrite, $NaNO_2$, to hydrochloric acid. Diazonium salts decompose above 10°C.

In the second step, the azo dye is formed by reacting the diazonium salt with a solution of 2-naphthol dissolved in $2\,mol\,dm^{-3}$ sodium hydroxide. The reaction mixture should be slightly alkaline in this stage.

$$C_6H_5N^+{\equiv}NCl^- + C_{10}H_7OH \rightarrow C_6H_5N{=}NC_{10}H_6OH + H^+ + Cl^-$$

Phenylamine is liquid at room temperature. Its density is $1.02\,g\,cm^{-3}$. It is carcinogenic and easily absorbed into the body through the skin, nose and lungs. It is also readily combustible.

2-naphthol is a solid at room temperature. It is harmful and is toxic to aquatic organisms. Sodium nitrite is toxic.

You are going to:

1 Plan an experiment to make a **small** sample of benzene-azo-2-naphthol

2 Answer questions about the procedure.

Equipment

Suggest suitable quantities of each reagent that should be used.

HINT
2-naphthol and nitrous acid should be in excess

Safety considerations

Describe what specific safety precautions should be taken in this experiment.

....

....

....

....

....

Method

Describe how you would carry out an experiment to make a sample of solid benzene-azo-2-naphthol

You should take into account that:

- Both nitrous acid and the diazonium salt formed in the first stage of the reaction are unstable when heated.

- The melting point of benzene-azo-2-naphthol is 131 °C.

....

....

....

....

....

....

....

………

………

………

Evaluation

a Give two reasons why the nitrous acid should be in excess.

………

………

b In the first stage, why should the sodium nitrite solution be added very slowly to the solution of phenylamine?

………

c How can you make sure that the procedure you suggested will be effective?

………

………

d The yields of benzene-azo-2-naphthol obtained can vary widely. Suggest why.

………

………

e Suggest how you could purify an impure sample of benzene-azo-2-naphthol.

………

………

………

f How could you check that your sample of benzene-azo-2-naphthol is pure?

………

………

g Most samples of phenylamine are yellowish in colour. What would you do to demonstrate that the colour formed was due to the azo-dye and not just due to a slow reaction of phenylamine with the nitrous acid?

………

………

………

h Suggest why you should not dispose of excess reagents down the sink.

....

....

Practical investigation 16.2: Data analysis
Acylation of a nucleic acid

Extension investigation

Introduction

Proteins and nucleic acids are natural polymers. They are synthesised in living organisms by a complex process. One stage in this process involves the attachment of amino acids to specific nucleic acids called transfer ribonucleic acids (tRNAs). The carboxylic acid group of the amino acid interacts with the tRNA and another molecule called ATP in an enzyme-catalysed reaction. During this process, the amino acid becomes attached to the tRNA by an acylation reaction.

$$\text{amino acid + tRNA} \xrightarrow{\text{enzyme}} \text{aminoacyl-tRNA}$$

The course of this reaction can be followed by using an amino acid in which a carbon atom is 'labelled' with a radioactive ^{14}C atom. As the reaction proceeds, more and more of the radioactive ^{14}C gets incorporated into the aminoacyl-tRNA. The radioactivity is measured by a radiation counter which measures the number of counts per minute of radioactive ^{14}C.

The specific enzyme which catalyses the acylation of the amino acid proline was isolated from the plant Delonix regia. The enzyme catalyses the reaction

$$\text{proline + tRNA} \rightarrow \text{prolyl- tRNA}$$

Experiments were carried out using proline containing a radioactive ^{14}C atom to determine the effect of pH on this enzyme-catalysed reaction. The concentration of the enzyme, proline, tRNA and ATP were kept constant in each case. The pH was varied by using a buffer containing varying volumes of maleic acid and tris(hydroxymethyl) aminomethane (commonly known as tris).

The reaction was carried out as follows:

- Place 3 cm^3 of the mixture of enzyme, tRNA and ATP in a test tube

- Add 5 cm^3 of buffer solution of known pH

- Add 2 cm^3 of radioactive proline and start the stopclock

- After 8 minutes add 1 cm^3 trichloroethanoic acid

- Filter off the solid produced (tRNA and protein) and record the number of counts of radioactivity per minute.

Data analysis

The results are shown Table 16.1:

Average background radiation during Run 1 = 6 counts / min

Average background radiation during Run 2 = 8 counts / min

pH	Run 1 Counts / min	Run 1 Corrected counts / min	Run 2 Counts / min	Run 2 Corrected counts / min	Average Corrected counts / min
5.80	10		12		
6.00	14		16		
6.15	21		42		
6.45	53		62		
6.60	68		75		
6.75	80		84		
6.95	91		89		
7.10	93		98		
7.25	96		100		
7.55	102		106		
7.85	106		112		
8.15	116		116		
8.75	114		116		
9.00	111		115		
9.50	104		118		
10.0	106		112		

Table 16.1

a   Complete Table 16.1.

b   Use the grid provided to plot a graph of average corrected counts / min against pH.

HINT
When drawing the line, you may need to consider two possible options

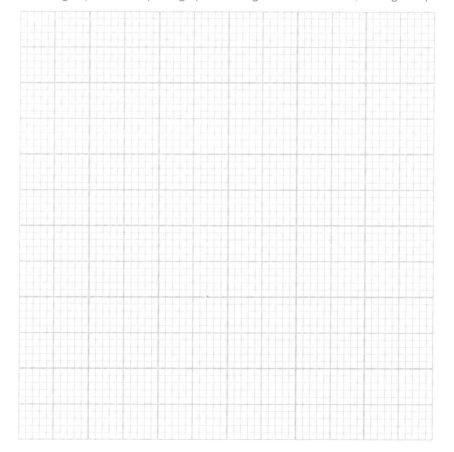

Evaluation

c What other factor should be kept constant during this experiment? Give a reason for your answer.

....

....

d Why is it necessary to take readings of background radiation?

....

....

e To what extent does the background radiation contribute to the inaccuracy of the experiment?

....

....

....

f What assumption has been made about the measurement of the radiation in counts / min? Explain why this is important.

....

....

g What is the purpose of the trichloroethanoic acid?

....

h Use your knowledge of the properties of amino acids to explain how the radioactive proline is separated from the radioactive tRNA.

....

....

i Describe the shape of the graph. What further experiments should you conduct to ensure that the graph is not a smooth curve but can be drawn as three more or less straight lines with differing gradients?

....

....

....

j What was the purpose of the buffer solution?

....

....

The graph shows a definite change in gradient at around pH 7. It has been suggested that this is linked to the enzyme having several subunits and several catalytic sites.

k Suggest one other reason for this change.

....

....

....

l Suggest why the experiment may not work if the enzyme extracted from the plant is not pure.

....

....

Practical investigation 16.3: Planning
Nitration of benzene

Introduction

Nitrobenzene is made by heating benzene with a mixture of concentrated nitric acid and sulfuric acid. The nitrating agent is the nitronium ion, NO_2^+, which is formed when nitric acid and sulfuric acid are mixed.

$$C_6H_6 + NO_2^+ \rightarrow C_6H_6NO_2$$

You are going to:

1 plan an experiment to make a small sample of nitrobenzene

2 suggest how to separate the product from the rest of the reaction mixture

3 answer questions about the procedure.

Use the following information to help you:

- Concentrated nitric acid (corrosive) has a density of $1.84\,g\,cm^{-3}$.

- Concentrated sulfuric acid (corrosive) has a density of $1.51\,g\,cm^{-3}$.

- Benzene (carcinogenic) has a density of $0.88\,g\,cm^{-3}$. About 0.08 mol benzene should be used.

- The reaction of benzene with a mixture of concentrated nitric acid and concentrated sulfuric acid is highly exothermic. The reaction between nitric acid and sulfuric acid is also highly exothermic.

- The reaction mixture should be heated at 60 °C for 30 minutes.

- Nitrobenzene is insoluble in water. Its density is $1.2\,g\,cm^{-3}$. Its boiling point is 210 °C.

- Water can be removed from an organic substance by shaking with sodium sulfate.

Equipment

Suggest suitable quantities of each reagent that should be used.

Method

Describe how you would carry out an experiment to make a sample of pure nitrobenzene.

You should consider how to obtain a sample of pure dry nitrobenzene from the reaction mixture. The sample should be free from acid.

....

....

....

....

....

....

....

....

....

....

Safety considerations

How would you carry out the reaction safely to obtain the product?

Evaluation

a Why should the mixture of sulfuric and nitric acids be in excess?

....

....

b Suggest why the reaction should not be carried out in a beaker.

....

....

c Corrosive vapours are formed during this experiment. Apart from using a fume cupboard, what features of your experiment helps minimise the production of these vapours?

....

....

....

d The yield of pure nitrobenzene is less than 70%. Suggest why the yield is not higher.

....

....

....

....

e How could you check that your sample of nitrobenzene is pure?

....

....

Chapter outline

This chapter relates to Chapter 29: Analytical chemistry in the coursebook.

In this chapter you will complete investigations on:

- 17.1 Extracting an amino acid from hair
- 17.2 Identification of a white crystalline solid
- 17.3 Preparation and identification of a colourless liquid

Practical investigation 17.1: Data analysis
Extracting an amino acid from hair

Introduction

Hair contains the protein keratin. An amino acid, **A**, can be extracted from keratin using the method given below.

In this investigation you will:

1   answer questions about the method used

2   identify the amino acid extracted from keratin.

Method

1   50 g of hair is weighed out and washed to free it of grease.

2   Heat the hair for 6 hours with concentrated hydrochloric acid.

3   Neutralise the solution and then adjust the pH to pH 5.

4   Allow the solution to stand overnight. A brown precipitate is formed.

5   Filter off the brown precipitate and boil with moderately concentrated hydrochloric acid.

6   Add powdered charcoal to the yellowish-brown solution and warm.

7   Adjust the solution to pH 5 and leave to form crystals.

8   Recrystallise the sample.

Data analysis

a   Name a suitable solvent for removing the grease in Step 1. Give a reason why you chose this solvent.

....

....

b Draw a labelled diagram of the apparatus you would use in Step 2.

c What is the purpose of Step 2?

....

....

d Describe how you would neutralise the solution in Step 3 and then adjust its solution to pH 5.

....

....

....

e Describe how you could obtain a pure dry sample of the crystals from Step 7.

....

....

....

f Describe how you would carry out recrystallisation.

....

....

....

A number of tests were carried out on amino acid A.
Answer the following questions about these tests.

A few drops of butanol were added to a concentrated solution of A. The mixture was heated gently.
A sweet smelling substance was formed.

g What functional group is likely to be present?

....

Use the internet or textbooks to find out about the Lassaigne test. Hydrochloric acid was added
to the solid obtained from heating A with sodium. A gas was given off which turned damp white
lead ethanoate paper brownish-grey.

h What conclusions can be drawn from this?

....

A solution of the solid obtained from heating A with sodium was made. To this solution was added a little solid iron(II) sulfate and a few drops of $2\,mol\,dm^{-3}$ sodium hydroxide. The solution was boiled for one minute and a few drops of acidified iron(III) chloride solution added and the solution filtered. Small blue particles of solid were seen on the filter paper.

i What conclusions can be drawn from this?

....

The results of paper chromatography carried out on a solution of A are shown in Figure 17.1 (using a solvent containing pyridine and water). The results show that the amino acid A is contaminated with a small amount of another amino acid.

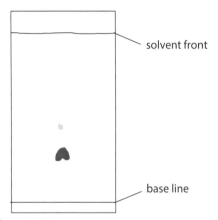

Figure 17.1

j Identify the amino acid A as well as the contaminating amino acid using the R_f values in Table 17.1. Show how you arrived at your answer.

Amino acid	Argine	Cystine	Glycine	Histidine	Lysine	Serine	Threonine
R_f value	0.25	0.28	0.44	0.42	0.22	0.51	0.60

Table 17.1

k Are the results of the chromatography conclusive? If not, explain why not and describe what you could do to get more conclusive results.

....

....

Practical investigation 17.2: Data analysis
Identification of a white crystalline solid

Introduction

Some information about three organic compounds **X**, **Y** and **Z** is given below. In this investigation you are going to answer questions about these organic compounds and identify compounds **X**, **Y** and **Z**.

1   **X** is a white solid having the formula $C_{13}H_{10}O_2$. **X** is hydrolysed with aqueous sodium hydroxide and the solution formed is neutralised with hydrochloric acid.

2   Two solids, **Y** and **Z**, are separated from this solution by fractional crystallisation.

3   **Y** reacts with bromine water to form a white precipitate.

4   **Y** is slightly soluble in water. A solution of **Y** turns Universal Indicator from green to yellowish-green. The solution does not react with sodium carbonate.

5   **Y** reacts with benzoyl chloride and sodium hydroxide to give compound **X**.

6   Solid **Z** is only very slightly soluble in water but reacts with aqueous sodium hydroxide to form a solution which conducts electricity and with aqueous sodium carbonate to produce carbon dioxide.

7   The mass spectrum (Figure 17.2) and infrared spectrum (Figure 17.3) of **Y** are shown.

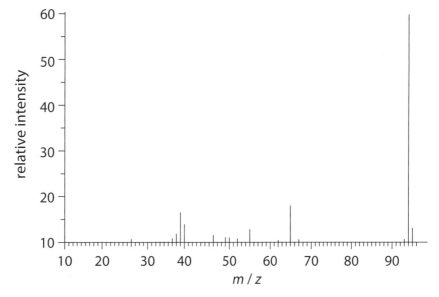

Figure 17.2

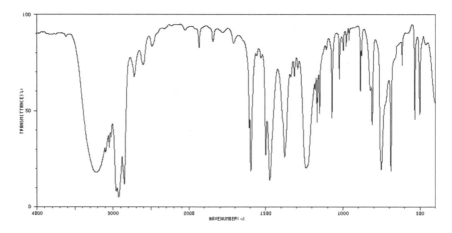

Figure 17.3

Data analysis

a Describe how to carry out the hydrolysis of compound **X**.

....

....

b What can be deduced about the properties of **Y** from point 4?

....

....

c Use the information in the mass spectrum to deduce the relative molecular mass of **Y**.

....

....

d Use the information from part **c** and points 3–5 to deduce the structure of **Y**. Give reasons for your answer.

....

....

....

....

....

....

e Use the information in Table 17.2 to suggest how the infrared spectrum of **Y** is consistent with your deduction in part **d**.

Bond	Location	Wavenumber / cm⁻¹
C–O	alcohols, esters	1000–1300
C=C	aromatic compounds, alkenes	1500–1680
C=O	aldehydes, ketones, carboxylic acid	1680–1750
C≡C	alkynes	2150–2250
C≡N	nitriles	2200–2250
O–H	hydrogen-bonded carboxylic acid	2500–3000 (broad)
C–H	CH$_2$–H in alkanes	2850–2950
C–H	=C–H in alkenes, arenes	2950–3100
O–H	hydrogen-bonded alcohols and phenols	3230–3550 (broad)
O–H	not hydrogen bonded	3580–3670

Table 17.2

....

....

....

....

f Describe the apparatus you would use to test for carbon dioxide in point 6. Give the positive result of this test.

....

....

....

g Deduce the structure and names of **Z** and **X**. Give reasons for your answer.

....

....

....

....

Practical investigation 17.3: Data analysis
Preparation and identification of a colourless liquid

Introduction

Some information about the preparation of a colourless organic liquid, **R**, is given. You will answer questions about this preparation and then attempt to identify this liquid.

Method

1   Liquid **R** is made by oxidising liquid **S** with a mixture of potassium dichromate(VI) and moderately concentrated sulfuric acid.

2   Liquid **R** has a boiling point of 78 °C; liquid **S** has a boiling point of 21 °C.

3   To start the reaction, a mixture of potassium dichromate(VI) and **S** is slowly added to sulfuric acid.

4   Only gentle heating is needed and the product **R** is then separated immediately from the reactants.

Data analysis

a   Draw a labelled diagram of the single set of apparatus you would use to prepare a sample of **R** in a safe manner.

b   Describe briefly how you would carry out the experiment.

    ....

    ....

    ....

    ....

    ....

    ....

Use this information about **R** to answer the following questions that follow.

- **R** reacts with an alkaline solution of copper(II) ions when warmed to form an orange–red precipitate.

- **R** reacts with tri-iodomethane to form a yellow precipitate.

- The mass spectrum (Figure 17.4) and infrared spectrum (Figure 17.5) of **R** are shown.

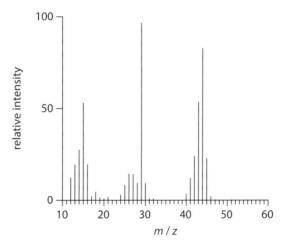

Figure 17.4

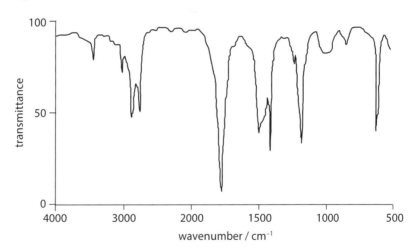

Figure 17.5

c   What does bullet point 1 tell you about the functional group present in **R**?

    ....

    ....

d   What does bullet point 2 tell you about **R**?

    ....

    ....

e Use the information in the mass spectrum to deduce the relative molecular mass of **R**.

....

....

f Account for the fragments of $\dfrac{m}{z}$ ratio 15 and 29 in the mass spectrum of **R.**

....

....

g Use the information from parts **a–f** to deduce the structural formula of **R**. Explain your answer.

....

....

....

h Use the information in Table 17.2 to suggest how the infrared spectrum of **R** is consistent with your deduction in part **g**.

....

....

i Deduce the structural formula of **S**.

....